experimentation with unfamiliar subject matter, as well as his deep sensitivity to criticism, caused his creative decline and ultimate paralysis.

William Inge, Revised Edition is the only comprehensive overview of the dramatist's life and work. A balanced retrospective of an important American playwright, *William Inge, Revised Edition* offers a penetrating look at the career of a gifted writer, haunted by his own success.

THE AUTHOR

R. Baird Shuman is a professor of English at the University of Illinois at Urbana-Champaign. His published works include *Clifford Odets, Robert E. Sherwood,* and *The First R: Fundamentals of Initial Reading Instruction.*

William Inge
Revised Edition

Twayne's United States Authors Series

Warren French, Editor
University of Wales, Swansea

TUSAS 95

WILLIAM INGE
1913–1973
Courtesy of the William Inge Collection, Independence Community College,
Independence, Kansas and of Helene Inge Connell.

William Inge

Revised Edition

By R. Baird Shuman

University of Illinois at Urbana-Champaign

Twayne Publishers
A Division of G. K. Hall & Co. • Boston

William Inge, Revised Edition

R. Baird Shuman

Copyright 1989 by G. K. Hall & Co.
All rights reserved.
Published by Twayne Publishers
A Division of G. K. Hall & Co.
70 Lincoln Street
Boston, Massachusetts 02111

First edition copyright © 1965, Twayne Publishers, Inc.

Copyediting supervised by Barbara Sutton
Book production by Gabrielle B. McDonald
Book design by Barbara Anderson

Typset in 11 pt. Garamond
by Williams Press, Inc. of Albany, New York

Printed on permanent/durable acid-free paper
and bound in the United States of America

Library of Congress Cataloging-in-Publication Data

Shuman, R. Baird (Robert Baird), 1929–
    William Inge / by R. Baird Shuman.—Rev. ed.
        p.   cm.—(Twayne's United States authors series ; TUSAS 95)
    Bibliography: p.
    Includes index.
    ISBN 0-8057-7537-4
    1. Inge, William—Criticism and interpretation.   I. Title.
II. Series.
PS3517.N265Z87   1989
812'.54—dc19   88-38550
                                                                                      CIP

For
Gideon Schlessinger,
a dependable friend who helped me
over some of the rough spots,
and for
Ahmed Mah'od Ali Al-Bdour
of
Yarmouk University in Irbid, Jordan,
whose literary understanding exceeds that
of
any scholar I have met

Contents

About the Author

R. Baird Shuman, professor of English at the University of Illinois at Urbana–Champaign, has previously taught at Duke University, San José State University, Drexel University, and the University of Pennsylvania. He has been visiting professor at the Bread Loaf School of English of Middlebury College, the University of Tennessee, Lynchburg College, East Tennessee State University, Olivet Nazarene University, the Philadelphia Conservatory of Music, and the Moore Institute of Art. Among the seventeen books he has written or edited are two Twayne volumes, *Clifford Odets* (1962) and *Robert E. Sherwood* (1964). He has served as executive editor of *The Clearing House* since 1975. His most recent book is *The First R: Fundamentals of Initial Reading Instruction* (1987), published by the National Education Association.

Preface

After Lloyd Steele interviewed William Inge for the Los Angeles *Free Press* shortly before the playwright's death in 1973, he decided to suppress the interview because it revealed a sad, disturbed William Inge, a William Inge convinced that he had lost his ability to write, a William Inge in the grip of a deep depression, a cancer of the spirit that he was powerless to shake.

When news of Inge's suicide on 10 June 1973 reached Steele, he was distressed but not surprised. He reconsidered his original judgment about publishing his William Inge interview, now the playwright's last. On 22 June 1973 the interview was run in the *Free Press*. It depicted a deeply troubled playwright who forgot that the interview had been scheduled, a man who slept as much as he could to obliterate his pain, perhaps to recover in his dreams some fragment of the more hopeful years of his life.

According to Steele, it took Inge several minutes to respond to his doorbell on the morning of the interview. He finally opened the door and, standing in his underwear, acknowledged the interviewer, squinting at Steele against the bright California sun, "absolutely pale, absolutely vulnerable." The accoutrements of Inge's financial success surrounded him—the lavish home above Sunset Boulevard, the swimming pool, the expensive furniture, the porcelain figurines, the period vases, the well-chosen paintings. The man Steele found in this setting, however, was a broken man struggling for survival but not really wanting to survive, a man who would never again know the magic of creativity, although this magic was the only meaningful ingredient in William Inge's life.

Steele reminded Inge that he had once likened the onset of his inspiration for a new piece of writing to the thrill fishermen feel when a fish strikes the line. But Inge mused that this kind of thrill now evaded him, complaining to Steele, "It's all false starts. Nothing but nibbles." Such were the feelings Inge, a truly gentle man, lived with for the final years of his life, the years after he had suffered the rejection of three Broadway plays in a row.

The first edition of this book was published soon after the second of Inge's failures, *Natural Affection* (1963), closed, having run for only three dozen performances. This revised edition reassesses the Inge plays I dealt with in my 1965 study and presents analyses of Inge's published work between *Natural Affection* and his death. This corpus of work includes his play, *Where's Daddy?*, his published novels, *Good Luck, Miss Wyckoff* (1970) and *My Son Is a Splendid Driver* (1971), and some of his later short plays, *The Call* (1968), *A Murder* (1968), and *The Disposal,* also entitled *The Last Pad* (1968).

In the late plays, Inge experimented with new themes and new techniques, but he did so only tentatively. *The Last Pad* is concerned with capital punishment, and has been revived frequently, although it has never played on Broadway. *The Call* and *The Murder* are interesting attempts at absurdist writing, perhaps in response to suggestions that *Where's Daddy?* (1966) could have succeeded had it been rewritten as an unabashedly absurdist play.

Inge's late experiments are promising works, but when one views them in relation to his novels, products of about the same period of his life, it becomes clear that Inge really wrote with greater conviction and enthusiasm about small towns in the Midwest and their effects upon people than he was able to muster for any other subject.

Good Luck, Miss Wyckoff presents many of the situations Inge dealt with in *Picnic* (1953), but in this later novel, he is more sexually explicit than he was in his earlier writing. *My Son Is a Splendid Driver* is a nostalgic work, essentially an autobiographical novel, a gentle reappraisal of many of the recurrent elements that pervaded Inge's life: Victorian prudery, Oedipus problems, the hypocrisy of the righteous, the torment of guilt, economic uncertainty.

My goal has been to present a balanced view of William Inge and his work and in a broader sense to show the inroads that celebrity and public expectations make upon the private and creative life of a sensitive, highly gifted person who suddenly is thrust into the spotlight. Inge did his best work when he wrote to satisfy his own expectations rather than those of brash, ambitious critics, some of whom not only failed to understand the midwestern milieu about which Inge wrote most vitally but who also had an evident antipathy for the area and the kinds of people upon whom Inge could most naturally and credibly focus his creative attention.

R. Baird Shuman

University of Illinois at Urbana–Champaign

Acknowledgments

I extend my deepest gratitude to William Inge and to his sister, Helene Inge Connell. Inge was extraordinarily cooperative in helping me to write my first book on him in 1965, and he kept me informed about his career in the years following that publication until his death in 1973. Upon his death, his sister continued to keep in touch with me, providing friendship and useful information about her brother in his final years.

When I began writing this book, I was visiting professor of English at the University of Tennessee, Knoxville, during the winter and spring quarters of 1987. Joseph B. Trahern, Jr., head of UTK's Department of English, and Edward Bratton, associate head, cooperated with my efforts by providing me with the sort of compact teaching schedule that left me blocks of time for research and writing. Other colleagues at Tennessee—Katherine Adams, Jack Armistead, Robert Drake, John Hurt Fisher, Nancy Goslee, Mary Richards, and Ralph Walker—helped in many ways, as did my students there, most notably Curtis Currie, Wynn Curtis, Eric Hobson, Don S. Lawson, and Mark Spurlock. The personnel of the University of Tennessee Library were unfailingly co-operative in helping me locate materials without which this book could not have been completed. Curtis White engaged me in interesting conversations about Inge.

Dale V. Kramer, acting head of the Department of English, and Richard Wheeler, head of the Department of English at the University of Illinois at Urbana–Champaign, arranged to release me for one semester from half my teaching load so that I could work on this book. For this consideration, I am deeply in their debt. Zohreh T. Sullivan of the University of Illinois has been an understanding and valued colleague to me as my work progressed, as has George Hendrick. I thank the staffs of the University of Illinois Library System and of the Champaign Public Library for working hard to help me meet my research needs.

Ralph Voss of the University of Alabama, who is writing a definitive biography of William Inge, shared valuable materials with me and made me realize fully what the word "collegiality" means. I value his willingness to cooperate with me. I also was accorded many courtesies by the editorial board of the *Kansas Quarterly*, which is composed of W. R. Moses, Ben Nyberg, John Rees, and Harold Schneider. *KQ* devoted its winter issue of 1986 to William Inge, and the editors saw to it that I quickly received a copy when I most needed it.

Richard S. Powers gave freely of his time to help me understand computers well enough to put my manuscript on disks. Carol Anne Moore transferred the manuscript to hard disk and printed the final copy for me. J. D. Daubs of the University of Indiana at Indianapolis and James P. Davis of Granville University also provided me with useful insights, as did Gideon Schlessinger of the University of Illinois.

I presented portions of this book at the Third Annual Literary Conference of the Department of English at Yarmouk University in Irbid, Jordan, in October 1987. I thank those who arranged for me to attend the conference, particularly Professors Mahmoud Shetawi, Mohammad Ajlouni, and Fares Mitleb. More particularly, I express my heartfelt thanks to Ahmed Mah'od Ali Al-Bdour, a brilliant undergraduate student at Yarmouk University, who provided me with literary insights so profound and incisive that I have viewed literature generally in a new light ever since I met him.

Del Singleton and Melissa Ruberson, curators of the William Inge Collection at Independence Community College in Independence, Kansas have given me free access to the collection and have been indispensable to me as my work progressed. A "Shoe-String" grant from the University of Illinois subsidized two trips to this valuable collection.

Liz Traynor of Twayne Publishers has been efficient in handling the details of getting this manuscript to press. I also owe a special debt to Warren French who read the manuscript and made a great many valuable suggestions to me for strengthening it.

Although I appreciate profoundly the efforts of all those who helped me bring this book to fruition, I must, of course, bear full personal responsibility for any errors of commission or omission that have crept into its pages.

Chronology

1913	William Motter Inge born 3 May in Independence, Kansas, the fifth and last child of Maude Sarah Gibson and Luther Clayton Inge.
1927–1930	Attends Montgomery County High School, Independence, Kansas.
1930–1935	Attends University of Kansas at Lawrence. Receives bachelor of arts degree in 1935.
1932	Acts in a Kansas tent show during the summer.
1933–1934	Drops out of the University of Kansas for a year and plays juvenile roles in tent shows.
1934	Works for the summer with the Maxinkuchee Mummers sponsored by Culver Military Academy in Indiana.
1935–1937	Attends George Peabody College for Teachers to study for master of arts degree in English. Leaves two weeks before graduation because of illness.
1936	Works on road gang in Kansas during the summer.
1936–1937	Works as news announcer and scriptwriter for radio station KFH in Wichita, Kansas.
1937–1938	Teaches English in the high school of Columbus, Kansas.
1938	Completes work for A. M. in English at George Peabody College for Teachers. Completes master's thesis entitled "David Belasco and the Age of Photographic Realism in the American Theatre."
1938–1943	Teaches English composition and drama at Stephens College, Columbia, Missouri.
1943–1946	Serves as art, music, book, and drama critic for the *St. Louis Star-Times*.
1945	Meets Tennessee Williams; writes first play, *Farther Off from Heaven*.
1946–1949	Teaches English at Washington University, St. Louis, Missouri.
1947	Margo Jones's Theatre 47 of Dallas, Texas, produces *Farther Off from Heaven*.
1949	Theatre Guild gives *Come Back Little Sheba* a tryout in Westport, Connecticut.

1950   *Come Back, Little Sheba* opens on Broadway and wins the George Jean Nathan Award.

1953   *Picnic* opens on Broadway. Inge receives Pulitzer Prize, Drama Critics' Circle Award, and Donaldson Award. Outer Critics' Circle votes *Picnic* the best play of 1953.

1955   *Bus Stop* opens on Broadway.

1957   *The Dark at the Top of the Stairs* opens on Broadway.

1959   *A Loss of Roses* opens on Broadway. *Four Plays by William Inge* published.

1960   British edition of *Four Plays* published.

1961   Inge's movie *Splendor in the Grass* is released and wins Academy Award for Best Original Script; Bantam Books publishes script.

1962   *Summer Brave and Eleven Short Plays.*

1963   *Natural Affection* opens on Broadway.

1964   *Out on the Outskirts of Town* airs on national television.

1965   Screen version of *Bus Riley's Back in Town* released.

1966   *Where's Daddy?* opens on Broadway.

1970   *Good Luck, Miss Wyckoff* published.

1971   British and paperback editions of *Good Luck, Miss Wyckoff* published. *My Son Is a Splendid Driver.*

1972   Writes "The Boy from the Circus," unpublished.

1973   Dies of carbon monoxide poisoning on 10 June. His death is ruled a suicide.

Chapter One
From the Heartland

America's heartland, its sprawling Midwest, has long engaged the interest and imaginative powers of America's most celebrated writers. In *Sister Carrie* and *Jennie Gerhardt,* Theodore Dreiser told the stories of two women who bolted in desperation from the monotony and narrow-mindedness of the heartland to find their fortunes in Chicago, the major metropolis most easily accessible to them. Edgar Lee Masters told in poetry the stories of some of the prominent townspeople who lay in the cemetery on the hill above Spoon River. Willa Cather recounted in many of her short stories and novels the lives of the pioneers who were homesteaders in Nebraska, and America's first Nobel laureate in literature, Sinclair Lewis, exposed in his novels the philistinism and hypocrisy of Gopher Prairie and Zenith. Sherwood Anderson revealed what went on behind the staid façades of the stately houses on the main street of Winesburg, Ohio, and Carl Sandburg celebrated in verse Chicago, hog butcher to the world.

Despite the sometimes condescending and cynical attention writers focused on the heartland, the relatively few dramatists who have turned their attention to the area have generally celebrated its wholesomeness rather than exposed its blemishes, as William Inge did. The most popular musical of the 1940s, *Oklahoma!* (based on Lynn Riggs's *Green Grow the Lilacs*), is set in the general area of most of Inge's early plays, but, as Robert Brustein wrote, Rodgers and Hammerstein's Oklahoma is "a joyous zone of calico gowns, scrubbed blue jeans, and homogenized souls."[1] Until Inge began to write dramas set in the Midwest, most of the drama set in that area presented midwesterners stereotyped either as a hearty breed of milkmaids and cowpokes, like those in *Oklahoma!,* or as people associated with the "brass bands, 'Ioway stubbornness,' and ingratiating con men" of Meredith Willson's *The Music Man.*[2]

Inge was the first successful playwright to examine the Midwest with psychological insight into what small-town life on the plains and the prairies did to people. He wrote about it seriously. He knew from having spent his first thirty-five years in the region what its sociological uniqueness was and how this uniqueness was revealed in the psychology of the people who lived there, particularly those who inhabited towns where everyone knew each other's business and where hypocritical standards of middle-class morality had a significant effect upon most of the citizens. Inge knew how to present with astounding veracity and authenticity the oppressive banality, the utter commonplaceness of the lives of his characters. The events in their daily lives occur and recur with the nerve-tightening regularity of a dripping faucet. Inge's female characters especially are overwhelmed by the bathos, repetitiveness, restraint, and futility of their lives. Inge capitalizes on the monotony of such existences to heighten dramatically the moment of personal crisis, the breaking point, that comes to all his major characters.

In his four major successes—*Come Back, Little Sheba; Picnic; Bus Stop;* and *The Dark at the Top of the Stairs*—Inge carries the audience through the moment of crisis, and his final curtain falls on a note of hope and fulfillment, however faint. Except for Madge in the stage version of *Picnic,* this hope and fulfillment come as a result of the protagonists' acceptance of life as it is, followed by an adjustment to what is clearly inevitable and a willingness to face life on less romantic terms than before.

The Early Years

William Inge was born on 3 May 1913 in Independence, Kansas, the last of five children of Maude Sarah Gibson and Luther Clayton Inge. He led the unexceptional life of a boy growing up in a sleepy midwestern town 160 miles south of Kansas City and some twenty miles north of the Oklahoma border. Luther Inge, a traveling salesman, was seldom home, and the young Inge grew up under the direct and overpowering influence of his mother, a puritanical woman of strong personality who dominated her husband and children. Bill was a bashful, retiring boy, much tied to his mother's apron strings.

His first interest in anything theatrical surfaced when he was seven or eight years old. His sister Helene was rehearsing a piece for recitation and Bill overheard her saying her lines. Shortly after that, quite un-characteristically, he jumped up in school and blurted out the lines he had heard his sister reciting. His classmates applauded this display of vitality, and his teacher apparently complimented him on it. Reflecting on the incident some thirty years afterward, Inge said that for the first time he had experienced audience reaction and that it had meant a great deal to him because it showed him a way to get along with people.[3] Soon afterward, young Bill Inge was doing recitations for civic and church groups.[4]

At about this time, Inge began to collect pictures of silent film stars and often, like Sonny Flood in *The Dark at the Top of the Stairs,* Inge found in these pictures a way to escape from the humdrum realities of his daily existence in Independence. Like Sonny Flood, also, Inge developed a cloyingly close relationship with his mother, attributable certainly to his father's long absences and to his being surrounded only by sisters, who became his closest companions. The contact with his mother provided the basis for his keen understanding of the mother–son relationships that he portrayed with insight in such plays as *The Dark at the Top of the Stairs, A Loss of Roses,* and *Natural Affection.*

The Inge play that draws most directly on the author's past is *The Dark at the Top of the Stairs.* The play is not wholly autobiographical, but in it the author clearly begins to come to grips with many of the fundamental psychological problems that faced him during adolescence and early adulthood. Inge, acknowledging that *The Dark at the Top of the Stairs* represented a new direction in his writing, called the play his first real attempt to examine his past and find meaning in it.[5] Although he scrupulously avoided emphasizing mother–son relationships in his first three Broadway plays, *Farther Off from Heaven,* which predates them and which is the basis for *The Dark at the Top of the Stairs,* his fourth play, touches tentatively on that subject.

Inge considered *Farther Off from Heaven* little more than a sketch.[6] He was not ready or able to achieve a deeper perspective until he had undergone psychoanalysis.[7] After extensive psychoanalysis, he was able to develop the oedipal theme in *The Dark at the Top of the Stairs.* He could now examine some of the darker sides of his own personality with an objectivity and dispassion that he previously lacked.

The Dark at the Top of the Stairs presents a psychological collage rather than an accurate autobiographical statement. Once Inge began to explore Sonny Flood's oedipal feelings, however, he moved on to explore the subject more deeply, particularly in *A Loss of Roses* and *Natural Affection,* as well as in the last novel he published, *My Son Is a Splendid Driver.*

Inge's boyhood in Independence was not much different from that of any other boy growing up in a small town in the Midwest during the 1920s, except that Inge was a mama's boy and was regarded by his schoolmates as a sissie. He was more sensitive and introspective than most boys of his age. Being the youngest child in a family dominated by women, Inge had been more protected than most children. Frequently in the company of his voluble mother, her talkative daughters, and his mother's ebullient sister, who is the prototype for Lola in *Come Back Little Sheba* and for Cora Flood in *The Dark at the Top of the Stairs*, the young Inge became a good listener, a shrewd judge of people and their speech patterns, and a perceptive observer of middle-class hypocrisy. These qualities, established early, served him well when he began to write plays.

Inge entered the Montgomery County High School in Independence in 1927. His major extracurricular activity was drama. Theater fascinated him, as it did his uncle, a frustrated actor, who sometimes took his nephew with him to see the performances of road companies in Kansas City.

Following graduation from high school in 1930, Inge entered the University of Kansas at Lawrence where he majored in speech and drama. He joined the university's theatrical troupe and wrote dialogue for its annual musical. During two of his summer holidays and during 1933–34, when he took a year off from his studies,[8] Inge played juvenile roles in touring Toby shows. As his years in Lawrence neared their end, he dreamed of going to New York City upon graduation to become an actor. His resolution to make the theater a central part of his life was fueled substantially by the experiences he had during the summer of 1933 when he worked with the Maxinkuchee Mummers sponsored by the Culver Military Academy in Indiana, to which he returned in the summer of 1935, after he had received the bachelor's degree, to teach and to save money so that he could go to New York to continue his career in drama.[9]

At about this time, however, Inge's family suffered financial reverses because of the Great Depression. He found himself without resources; his future prospects were limited. His work with touring companies had shown him how uncertain an actor's life can be. He now saw no way to go to New York. He knew it would be a dire mistake to return to Independence, where he would again fall under his mother's domination. When the George Peabody College for Teachers in Nashville, Tennessee, awarded him a scholarship to study for a master's degree in English, Inge accepted the offer and began graduate studies.

As Inge began his work in Nashville, his mind and heart were in New York. The conflict between what he was doing and what he wished he was doing frustrated him. He suffered from depression during his time at Peabody, and eventually suffered a nervous collapse so severe that he had to leave school two weeks short of his scheduled commencement in 1936. Inge, having based his life on the theater, returned to Kansas and floundered.[10]

Actually, Inge's floundering, although it was intense, was invaluable to him. It forced him to consider the purpose and future course of his life. As he moved toward a better understanding of his problems, he found that physical exhaustion was good for him, so in the summer of 1936, he took a job as a laborer with a Kansas road gang. Working vigorously for long hours under the searing Kansas sun renewed his strength and vitality.

By autumn Inge had regained his mental and physical tone. With the theater still foremost in his mind, he took a job in Wichita as a scriptwriter and announcer for radio station KFH. This work gave him an outlet related, however tenuously, to the world of theater that he coveted. Remaining active in amateur acting companies, he now seemed able to put aside his thoughts of becoming a Broadway actor and to tolerate his situation.

By 1938 a change had come over William Inge. He had never suffered from self-consciousness or stage fright when he appeared before theater audiences. When he played the role of choirmaster in a performance of Thornton Wilder's *Our Town,* however, he was so self-conscious and terrified that he vowed never to act again.[11] As distressing as this decision was for him, it marked an emancipation of sorts from the dream that had until now prevented him from finding the real course in his life. It took him eight more years to find his true direction, but freezing up in the Wilder play marked his turning point.

During the next years, Inge waited. Had he calculatedly planned these years, he probably could not have shaped them more specifically to achieve his ultimate ends than they did. What lay ahead led directly to Inge's emergence as a serious playwright.

The Teaching Years

Having finished most of his work for his M.A. before he left George Peabody College for Teachers in 1936, Inge was permitted to complete his degree off campus by writing a master's thesis. In 1937, he began to teach English in the high school of Columbus, Kansas. He liked his position well enough that he was now strongly motivated to complete his thesis, "David Belasco and the Age of Photographic Realism in the American Theatre," and get the degree.

By the summer of 1938, Peabody had accepted Inge's thesis, and Stephens College for Women in Columbia, Missouri, hired him to teach English. Besides freshman composition, Inge taught courses in drama and play production. He remained at Stephens for five years and found particularly rewarding close contact with his colleague, Maude Adams, grande dame of American theater and head of Stephens's Drama Department, whose enthusiasm for theater matched Inge's. He admired Adams's intelligence and envied her experience. Although Adams and Inge's closest faculty friends, Albert and Virginia Christ-Janer, made his years at Stephens more rewarding than they might otherwise have been, Inge realized that he was misplaced in teaching.[12]

Had it not been for the entry of the United States into World War II in 1941, Inge might have continued to teach unenthusiastically at Stephens and might never have become a playwright. In 1943, when the *St. Louis Star-Times* lost Reed Hynds, its drama, music, art, book critic, to the armed services, the newspaper offered Inge,[13] who had a deferment, the opportunity to take Hynds's place. Although the job was an overwhelming one, Inge accepted it and held it from 1943 until Hynds returned to it early in 1946. Inge held only one more teaching job before he devoted himself exclusively to his writing. In 1946, his stint at the *Star-Times* finished, he went to Washington College in St. Louis to teach English, a job he kept until 1949.

The *St. Louis Star-Times*

Inge realized that the position he accepted at the *Star-Times* offered him little security because it had to be held open for Reed Hynds. He knew that when the war ended, he would likely be competing for jobs with a deluge of returning veterans. His devotion to the theater was so great, however, that he would not let practical considerations block his way when he had the opportunity to become a drama critic. The position on the *Star-Times* finally catapulted Inge into his career as playwright. Even though he returned to teaching for three years after he left the newspaper, he was now securely on the way to becoming a playwright.

Until Inge joined the *Star-Times* in 1943, he had done only desultory writing, a few short stories and some poems. His master's thesis was the longest piece of sustained writing he had attempted. Writing dialogue for musicals when he was an undergraduate had made him aware of some of the demands of theatrical writing, but it is not this kind of writing that turned him into a playwright. Until now, he had not developed the fluency to write anything as comprehensive as a full-length play.

During his three years with the *Star-Times,* Inge wrote 417 reviews[14] on a range of topics so diverse that he became adept at changing gears instantly and at turning out finished copy against pressing deadlines. He usually was assigned reviews, but often he assumed the initiative for finding suitable feature story subjects for the newspaper. It was his quest for such a feature story that changed his life inalterably and led directly to his becoming a playwright.

Inge and Tennessee Williams

Inge first met Tennessee Williams in the fall of 1944, when Williams's *The Glass Menagerie* was in rehearsal for its break-in performance in Chicago. The play opened late in December of that year. Williams was in Clayton, on the outskirts of St. Louis, in his parents' modest suburban home trying to overcome the shock of instant celebrity when Inge called him to request an interview. He told Williams that "he did feature stories on theatrical folk passing through St. Louis and [that] he would like to do a sort of 'Home-town Boy Makes Good' article on me."[15] The two found that they shared common interests and developed an instant rapport.

In his introduction to Inge's *The Dark at the Top of the Stairs,* Williams recalls the kindly young man who interviewed him: "[Inge wondered] if I would not enjoy a little social diversion other than that provided by family friends in St. Louis, since my own small group of associates in the city had scattered far and wide, by this time, like fugitives from a sanguinary overthrow of state."[16] Williams and Inge met in this way, and their friendship through the years was a curious one. Williams, at first supportive of Inge, became jealous of his success, particularly when some of Inge's successful plays were on Broadway at the same time as some of Williams's failures, such as *Camino Real,* which had a run of sixty performances in 1953, and *Orpheus Descending,* which ran for about the same number of performances in 1957.

Williams told friends that he hoped Inge would not be awarded any prizes for *The Dark at the Top of the Stairs,*[17] a play that ironically is based on *Farther Off from Heaven,* which Williams initially arranged for Margo Jones, proprietor of the Dallas 47 Theater, to see. Williams renewed his friendship with Inge, however, in Inge's later years and gave advice to Inge's sister, Helene Connell, about how to deal with the depression, alcoholism, and drug dependence that were becoming such a problem to Inge.[18]

Shortly after Williams returned to Chicago to do further work on *The Glass Menagerie* before its opening on Broadway, Inge went to the city to see the play with Williams. The performance moved Inge to call it the finest play he had seen in years.[19] It made him realize that common people in ordinary settings are the stuff of which moving drama can be made, perhaps the most valuable lesson he learned from Williams,[20] to whom he now revealed his own desire to become a playwright.[21] During his visit to Williams in Chicago, their friendship developed into an intense but short-lived romance.[22] Williams, thinking that perhaps Inge had just been carried away by the enthusiasm of the moment, was not sure his friend was serious about wanting to become a playwright. Inge recalls, however, that he went back to St. Louis determined to write a play.[23]

Within three months, Inge had completed *Farther Off from Heaven*. At Williams's urging, he sent the play to Margo Jones, who was about to produce Williams's *Summer and Smoke* at her Dallas 47 theater. Inge had met Margo Jones when he went to Chicago to see *Glass Menagerie*. She agreed to produce his play in the summer of 1947.

In Dallas for the opening of his play, Inge realized he was destined to be a playwright. He returned to Washington University with the conviction that he would not teach there much longer but would soon be in a position to pursue his career on Broadway. Inge had grown to hate his teaching,[24] and he began to drink so heavily that in 1948 he had to turn to Alcoholics Anonymous for help. Although he did not overcome the drinking problem, he learned enough about alcoholism through his association with Alcoholics Anonymous that he was able to depict with flawless accuracy Doc Delaney's alcoholism in his first Broadway production, *Come Back, Little Sheba*.

Four Successive Triumphs

By early 1949 the one-act play that Inge had intended to write about Doc and Lola Delaney based on one of his unpublished short stories had blossomed into a full-length, two-act play in six scenes. Inge knew that *Come Back, Little Sheba* was a more mature play than *Farther*

Off from Heaven, which he felt suggested rather than explored the deeper meaning of life.[25] In the earlier play, of course, Inge had dealt with problems that he had not come to grips with until he was well into his psychoanalysis.[26]

Tennessee Williams was visiting in St. Louis when Inge finished *Come Back, Little Sheba.* During a visit to Inge's neo-Victorian white frame house on Maryland Avenue near Washington University, Williams recalls that Inge "shyly produced a play he had written" and read it aloud. Much moved by the play, Williams wired his New York agent, Audrey Wood, about it. When she read the play, she liked it as much as Williams had. She agreed to represent Inge.[27]

On 9 February 1949, Audrey Wood submitted *Come Back, Little Sheba* to the Theatre Guild, and within four days she had a preliminary report from the Guild that said the play at first seemed slight, but that its little touches made it grow on those who read it. The readers felt that in *Sheba,* Inge was playing out Thoreau's theory that all people live lives of quiet desperation.[28]

The Theatre Guild optioned *Come Back, Little Sheba* in the middle of March 1949, and the Equity reading of the play was held on 5 April 1949. The reaction was so favorable that Inge decided to resign from his teaching job at Washington University and go to New York and oversee the play's production. The play opened before a disparate postsummer audience in Westport, Connecticut on 12 September 1949 with Shirley Booth as Lola and Sidney Blackmer as Doc. The audience was unusually enthusiastic, repeatedly calling at the end of the performance for both cast and author and giving them prolonged ovations. Even though the summer season was over, *Come Back, Little Sheba* played before full houses for its week-long postseason run in Westport. The play seemed sure to be a hit on Broadway. However, Shirley Booth, whose Lola is still credited as one of the finest performances in American theater, seemed crucial to the play's success, and she had another Broadway commitment to fulfill during the fall season. After her resounding success as Lola in Westport, the Theatre Guild was reluctant to risk having someone else play Lola on Broadway. Inge agreed with the Guild's decision, which meant that the play could not go into rehearsals until 2 January 1950. The Guild scheduled it to open in Wilmington, Delaware, on 26 January and in Boston four days later.

The delay in bringing the play to Broadway took a significant toll on Inge. The strain of getting the play ready for production caused him to suffer a major nervous crisis that was complicated by his heavy drinking. He had to be hospitalized and, according to Williams, he could not attend the opening Broadway performance.[29] During this uncertain period, Inge was unable to proceed with any new projects and was in a state of limbo, drinking heavily and worrying.

The reviews of the out-of-town performances of *Come Back, Little Sheba* were mixed, but nearly all the critics, regardless of what fault they found with the play and its production, commended Inge's writing. Those who would not go so far as to call Inge a brilliant playwright conceded that he was highly competent and had a promising future.

The culmination of all Inge had been working for came when *Come Back, Little Sheba* opened at the Booth Theater in New York City on 15 February 1950. Shirley Booth, Sidney Blackmer, and their supporting cast were superb in the premier Broadway performance. The New York critics were generally favorable in their comments about the play, although all had reservations similar to those of Brooks Atkinson of the *New York Times,* who, in an overall favorable review, called the play artfully planned, but tight and narrow. A small group of critics was negative in its comments, but the play received sufficient favorable comment and enthusiastic audience reaction that it seemed assured of a reasonable run.

Sheba played for 190 performances, and during the first six weeks of its run, the theater was packed. When audiences began to dwindle, the actors took a cut in salary and Inge took a reduced royalty to keep the play going.[30] By most standards used to measure the success of a first play, *Sheba* was a triumph. It received four votes for the Drama Critics' Circle's best play of the 1949–50 season.

The sale of the play to Paramount Films, which released it in 1953 as a film starring Shirley Booth and Burt Lancaster, gave the play's backers a decent return on their investment. The Theatre Guild on the Air did a version of *Sheba* for radio, and the Guild was sufficiently pleased with Inge's work that on 1 October 1950, it took an option on his next play.

Inge was well aware of the hazards that face an author whose career begins too well. He began to worry about what he would do next. Insecurity gnawed at him as *Sheba* came to the end of its run. Less than a week before its last Broadway performance, Inge wrote that it is unfair to a writer to measure him against what is judged his best work because to do so deprives artists of their freedom. He complains that when writers are judged in this way, their work loses its personal value and becomes a mass experience, which he likens to a bullfight or a convention.[31] It is common for new playwrights to slink off and lick the wounds the critics or indifferent audiences have inflicted, but Inge had to face the greater problem of being forced to live up to the standard *Sheba* had established for him. The burden of this responsibility weighed heavily on him.

In 1946, Inge wrote a play called *Front Porch,* which the Experimental Group of the St. Louis Community Players planned to produce that year. The Experimental Group folded, however, before the play was put on, and it was not until 10 February 1948 that the Morse Players, under the aegis of Jack Balch, then a reviewer for the *St. Louis Post Dispatch,* produced it. During its two-week run, it played to full houses in the hundred-seat Toy Theater.[32]

The play's basic theme enthralled Inge, and he now decided to begin redrafting this somewhat inchoate manuscript into a finished play for Broadway. Retitled *Picnic,* the play brought its author a Pulitzer Prize, the New York Drama Critics' Circle Award, and the Donaldson Prize in 1953.

In the summer of 1950, when Inge began to rework *Front Porch,* he needed to escape from what he called the gloomy interior of *Sheba.*[33] He wanted his new play to take place in the sunshine, and he wanted one of the main characters to have the kind of surging vitality and overt sexuality he had noticed in members of the Kansas road gang he had worked with in the summer of 1936.

The play, which he tentatively called "Women in Summer," began as a series of dramatic sketches about women. From this gallery Inge created his drama. He had to grapple only briefly with giving dramatic intensity to his work. He decided to bring into the midst of his gallery of women a sexually tempting youth.[34] His instinct was good, and his creation of Hal, a muscular, dumb but lovable lout, immediately established the tension the play needed. Even though Inge's Adonis spent only a day among the women, his sheer animal magnetism pervaded their lives—and the play—totally.

The version of *Picnic* that Inge considered final was performed in Hyde Park, New York, in August 1952 as *Summer Brave,* certainly an ironic title. Before the play opened at the Music Box Theatre in New York City on 19 February 1953, Joshua Logan, its director, had convinced Inge to change the title and to make significant substantive changes in the script. Rehearsals became so painful for Inge, who was constantly being called upon to make decisions about changing the script, that he often left the theater in despair at what his play was becoming. Nevertheless, he had great respect for Logan. He knew that Logan's only desire was to make the play marketable, and although it troubled him to tamper with the script, he respected Logan's judgment enough to follow his advice.[35]

Picnic's opening night was more distressing for Inge than anything he had experienced up until then because his reputation was fully on the block, and he had fought too hard for that reputation to risk it with equanimity. However, he had little to fret about. Both the critical and the public response were gratifying, and the play, starring Ruth McDevitt and Ralph Meeker, ran for 477 performances. The prizes it won affirmed the enthusiastic critical reception *Picnic* received. Even critics who did not like the play called its craftsmanship impressive. Columbia Pictures promptly bought the movie rights on terms favorable to Inge and his backers. In 1956, Columbia released the film with an all-star cast that included William Holden, Rosalind Russell, Kim Novak, Betty Field, and Susan Strasberg.

Despite the success and acceptance *Picnic* brought to Inge, he did not have the kind of self-confidence that one expects to find in a successful playwright. He fretted because *Picnic* was a reworking of material he had written earlier. He wondered whether he was going to be able to create new material, particularly now that he had to deal with the demands and pressures that accompany success. Concerns about his ability to continue to create new material plagued him until his dying day and contributed to his suicide.

For his next play, Inge again turned to material he had written earlier. *Bus Stop* was an expansion of *People in the Wind,* a one-act play that Inge wrote in 1953. The play, reminiscent of Robert Sherwood's *The Petrified Forest* and, in some respects, of W. Somerset Maugham's *Rain,* opened at the Music Box Theatre on 2 March 1955 under the extremely sensitive direction of Harold Clurman, whom Inge considered the only real intellectual in theater.[36] *Bus Stop* ran until 21 April 1956, when it closed after 478 performances. It received critical acclaim, evoking praise such as that from *Time's* reviewer, who called it "the season's and possibly the author's best play."[37] Twentieth Century-Fox bought the film rights and rushed *Bus Stop* into production, releasing the film in 1956 with Marilyn Monroe playing Cherie, perhaps her most celebrated role.

Bus Stop's story line is just sufficient to provide the mortar that holds together the carefully studied and well-conceived character sketches of which the play is largely composed.[38] In this play, both in its one-act and extended versions, Inge created his gallery of characters quite autonomously at first and then welded these character sketches into a dramatic unity. In most of his early plays, Inge began his writing with characters rather than plots in mind, and once his characters were clearly established, he shaped his dramatic action around them.

Tennessee Williams thought that Inge wrote better dialogue than he,[39] and, although one might quarrel with Williams's contention, it is hard to deny that Inge's dialogue captures the authentic cadences and tone of the midwestern American vernacular, which is perhaps attributable to his initial concern with shaping his characters. In *Bus Stop,* Inge achieves focus and dramatic unity first by bringing his characters together in the microcosm the small restaurant provides and then by presenting these characters at a critical and decisive time in their lives. *Bus Stop* was more than a reworking of old materials. *People in the Wind* had been the barest of sketches, a mere suggestion of the fully realized drama that *Bus Stop,* with its complex revelation of human personality and group interaction, became.

As early as July 1953, Inge had thought of reworking *Farther Off from Heaven* into a new play.[40] He also planned to do a one-act play that he hoped would become a musical about some rodeo cowboys in New York. Remarkably dependable about carrying out his plans, Inge pursued them in this case just about as he had outlined them. His play about rodeo cowboys in New York became a play about Bo and Cherie. Turning *People in the Wind* into *Bus Stop* represented the fulfillment of the statement he had made two years before. Now he carried through on his other plan and began his concentrated reworking of *Farther Off from Heaven.*

The resultant play, *The Dark at the Top of the Stairs,* opened at the Music Box Theatre on 5 December 1957, directed by Elia Kazan. Actually, Inge had been working in a desultory manner on this play for six years, but it was not until the winter of 1957 that the play reached its final form. Inge wrote it with greater assurance than he had achieved in most of his previous writing. He by now had developed confidence about his craftsmanship.[41]

The suicide that takes place in *Dark* bothered some of the critics, but the play was well received critically, and it soon appeared certain that Inge had his fourth Broadway success in as many tries, a remarkable record for a playwright to achieve in a decade. When the play finally closed its Broadway run of 468 performances on 17 January 1959, critics and playgoers alike marveled at the success of a dramatist who wrote modest plays about prosaic people, but who had yet to experience a box-office failure.

It was obvious to those who thought about it that Inge's plays succeeded because of the strength of his characterization and dialogue rather than because of the excellence of his dramatic structure. In his ability to depict mundane, everyday characters who had a sense of universality about them, Inge achieved in theater what Charles Dickens had achieved in the best of his novels. The major difference between the way the two depicted character is that Dickens achieved his effects by overelaboration, whereas Inge generally underplayed his characters. Whereas many of Dickens's characters emerge as memorable caricatures, Inge's emerge as believable—and equally memorable—humans.

Dark marked the end of a significant phase in Inge's development both personally and as a playwright. Inge now left behind him the multiple successes of the 1950s and passed into a period of personal and artistic crisis.

The End of an Era

William Inge was convinced that *A Loss of Roses* was his best play. Even before it opened, Twentieth Century-Fox had paid $200,000 for the film rights, and it released the film in 1963 as *The Stripper,* starring Joanne Woodward and Gypsy Rose Lee. Inge put into the play half the money he received for the film rights. The original production cost $125,000.

Inge had reason to be optimistic about *A Loss of Roses.* It was his first wholly original script since *Sheba.* For Inge, the new play represented visible proof of his ability to produce fresh, new material. Also, on a psychological level, the new play represented a logical continuation of his exploration of the oedipal problem, which he had presented with some success in *Dark.* In the earlier play the problem was suggested; in the new play, it was presented full blown. This was perhaps why both critics and audiences rejected the play.

A Loss of Roses went into rehearsal with Shirley Booth as Helen Baird. Booth suggested significant changes in the script, and Inge acceded to many of them even though he feared these changes would weaken the play. Immediately after the Washington opening of the play, feeling that her role of Helen Baird was overshadowed by that of Lila Green, played by Carol Haney, Booth withdrew from the cast. She was replaced in New Haven by Betty Field, a fine actress, but one whom Inge thought was not right for the role. Field had had so little time to rehearse that her performance was not up to her usual standard. Before the New Haven run ended, Inge knew that he should close the show, revise the script extensively, pursue an intense schedule of rehearsals, and open on Broadway six weeks later, after the Christmas holidays. By this time, however, he had invested so much of his capital in the production that the cost of pursuing the indicated course would have devastated him financially. On 28 November 1959, *Loss* opened on schedule at the Eugene O'Neill Theatre under the direction of Daniel Mann, who had earlier produced *Sheba.* A play that Inge hoped would be added to his string of Broadway successes turned out to be a total catastrophe, the effects of which devastated its author.

When the first reviews appeared the morning after the Broadway opening, Inge was incredulous. He had anticipated that the play might not be well received, but he was not prepared for the tone of most of the reviews, which could be characterized only as personally vengeful and vindictive. On reading the reviews, Inge commented that he was being treated like someone who had spit on the floor.[42] It seemed to him that some of the critics had been waiting for him to write an inferior play so that they could abuse him. They were essentially telling him he did not have the right to create a play like *Loss.*

Badly shaken by what he perceived to be the utter cruelty of many of the critics, Inge fled from New York. He drove his convertible to Nashville, where he attempted to sort out his reactions to the debacle he had left behind. *Loss* closed on 19 December 1959 after twenty-five performances. Inge decided to turn his talents to something new, and as he tried to evaluate the failure of his play, he went to Florida for a vacation and began work on his first film script, *Splendor in the Grass,* which Twentieth Century-Fox released in 1961 starring Natalie Wood and Warren Beatty. The film script won Inge his only Oscar.

So encouraged was Inge by the success of *Splendor in the Grass* that he moved to California and did a second scenario, *All Fall Down,* adapted from the James Leo Herlihy novel. Metro-Goldwyn-Mayer released the film in 1962 with a stellar cast including Eva Marie Saint, Warren Beatty, Karl Malden, Angela Lansbury, and Brandon De Wilde. The film was entered in the prestigious Cannes Film Festival. The next film on which Inge worked, *That Hill Girl,* was never produced.

When Inge began to work in Hollywood, he suffered from the same sense of sin that had afflicted Clifford Odets when he left New York to begin writing for a different medium. But, whereas Odets went west voluntarily in 1937 to make money that he sent back to keep the Group Theatre afloat, Inge felt he had been pushed rudely from the nest. His reaction was a transparent rationalization that he found New York claustrophobic, that it was too big for him to prosper there creatively.[43]

Once Inge got to Hollywood, he threw himself into writing film scripts and into adapting to life in California. He recognized, however, the artistic compromises that were involved in scriptwriting, and he lived through a personal crisis caused by his own insecurities, by his inability to come to grips with his homosexuality, and by his sense that he was being compromised as an artist. The feeling of futility he felt when *Loss* was badly received grew stronger when his next play, *Natural Affection*, was not well received either on the road in 1962 or on Broadway in 1963. He moved back to New York in 1963 to work on *Bus Riley's Back in Town*, a film that Universal released in 1965. Inge was so displeased with the final script that, at his insistence, the credits did not list him as the author but rather attributed the screenplay to Walter Gage, a pseudonym he selected.

By 1965, Inge was again living in California, where he remained for the rest of his life. A final Broadway play, *Where's Daddy?*, opened at the Billy Rose Theatre on 2 March 1966 and ran for twenty-one performances. The harsh criticism that had followed *Loss* and *Affection* was repeated in the reviews of *Where's Daddy?*, and Inge began to consider it unlikely that he would ever have another Broadway success.

Inge on Modern Drama

Inge once said that a writer's first need is to please him- or herself. He knew that playwrights cannot succeed merely by pandering to the ephemeral tastes of their audiences. He feared that in the United States playwrights are resented for the very illumination they bring to life. Inge believed that a playwright should never ask his audiences to side with him because people come to the theater to discover something for themselves rather than to be lectured to.[44]

In an interview after *Picnic* had won several prizes, Inge said, "A play should be admired for the experiences it gives, not for the idea a playgoer comes away remembering. [The playgoer] should feel richer within himself, more responsive, more aware."[45] Inge liked to think his plays changed, however slightly, the way his audiences lived their lives.

In most of his plays, Inge writes about love, and the highest expression of love as Inge sees it often comes when someone realizes that non-judgmental, accepting love is the only kind that really endures. It is this sort of love that brings the main characters in many of Inge's plays a sense of ultimate fulfillment.

Although pervasive themes recur in Inge's plays, Inge declared, "I have never written a play that had any intended theme or that tried to propound any particular idea. . . . I want my plays only to provide the audience with an experience which they can enjoy (and people can enjoy themselves crying as much as laughing) and which shocks them with the unexpected in human nature, with the deep inner life that exists privately behind the life that is publicly presented."[46] In much that he wrote about theater, Inge admonished playwrights to grow beyond their work and not to be possessive of it,[47] a lesson he learned painfully when his own plays were in production.

After he had lived through the commercial failure of three of his plays, Inge, in 1967, concluded that lack of stimulation is "a serious problem in the American theater: it's no place to grow up in. New York wants the first flashy efforts, the sensations. . . . The artist himself, the way he matures and grows, is of no concern." He was no more sanguine about writing for Hollywood: "A writer may be able to work there for a short time if he's got a unique idea with commercial possibilities. To spend your life just writing for movies is like training yourself to become an expert secretary."[48] Inge grappled with these problems until his final days, when they overwhelmed him.

Inge's Final Years

Inge suffered great inner turmoil in the final decade of his life. He had suffered earlier from anxieties sufficient to bring on nervous collapses, some so severe that he required hospitalization. In these later years, when his sister Helene lived with and attended him, his sense of futility was almost unbearable.

As Broadway increasingly rejected his plays, Inge, who now taught playwriting sporadically at the Irvine Campus of the University of California and at the Actors and Directors Laboratory,[49] turned his fading energies to writing novels. His first novel, *Good Luck, Miss Wyckoff*, was published in 1971 by Atlantic/Little, Brown, and later that year, the same company published his second, highly autobiographical novel, *My Son Is a Splendid Driver*.

Although the first of these novels contains some demonstrably bad writing, its story line is strong. In this book, Inge returns to a theme he explored in *Sheba* and, more overtly, in *Picnic*. A sexually frustrated woman, Evelyn Wyckoff, a high school teacher in Freedom, a small Kansas town modeled on Inge's birthplace, Independence, is a thirty-seven-year-old virgin. She desperately wants and needs sex, which she ultimately finds with a young, black community college athlete, Rafe, who cleans up her classroom every day after school. When she lingers after school one day to grade papers, Rafe leaves Miss Wyckoff little choice but to yield to his blatant advances. When their affair comes to be known publicly, Miss Wyckoff is drummed out of town to an uncertain future, a lonely, rejected figure, as Inge felt himself to be at the time.

Despite the book's shortcomings, many of the critics reviewed it more gently than the drama critics had reviewed his plays after *Dark*. Some called the book technically competent, but felt that Inge had dealt with similar problems more effectively in his plays.[50] Others commented on his seeming discomfort in writing the explicit sex scenes that are necessary to the story's development. No major critic went so far as to comment on the faulty use of language in the book, even though it is this problem as much as any other that keeps *Good Luck, Miss Wyckoff* from realizing the potential inherent in its story.

My Son Is a Splendid Driver is essentially a memoir of a sensitive college English teacher, who thinks back on his family and his youth. Joey Hansen, enough like William Inge to be his clone, has always lived in the shadow of his older brother, the splendid driver referred to in the book's title. This brother is the mother's favorite, and when he dies shortly after his marriage to the girl across the street, the victim of blood poisoning brought on by a razor cut, the whole family loses hope. *My Son Is a Splendid Driver* is much better written than *Good Luck, Miss Wyckoff,* and in it Inge clearly moves in a promising new literary direction.

Shortly before the publication of his two novels, Inge had written a few one-act plays, of which *The Call* (1968), *A Murder* (1968), *The Disposal* (1968), and *Midwestern Manic* (1969) are in print. In January 1969, his play *Overnight,* which remains unpublished, was presented by a group at the University of California at Los Angeles.

The pessimism that overwhelmed Inge at this time is reflected consistently in his later writing. Inge's was a pessimism of long standing. In 1963, he said that he wished he could just write his plays and, because Broadway productions are such painful experiences, send them off to the moon to be produced. He felt that modern life is simply not designed to help creative people survive.[51] This sort of pessimism pervades the last interview Inge gave, only days before his death, to Lloyd Steele.[52] In this interview it is obvious that Inge had abandoned all hope. Early in June 1973, he was admitted to the UCLA Medical Center for psychiatric observation after he had tried to end his life with a drug overdose. He was released from the hospital after a few days, returning to the home he shared with his sister Helene. It was she who found him in their garage behind the wheel of his automobile, dead of carbon monoxide poisoning, in the predawn hours of 10 June 1973. On the table in their living room was an unopened brown envelope containing the typescript of Inge's latest novel, "The Boy from the Circus," which a New York publisher had rejected.

On the first anniversary of Inge's death, his sister wrote, "I miss him so very much, and can't help thinking *why*. Even though he had told me *why*. Mainly that he could not write anymore, and that was his only interest in life."[53] Inge had often expressed his fear of writer's block,[54] and, although his continuing productivity seems to negate his being a victim of it, his own perception was that he could write no more.

Chapter Two

Riding the Crest of the Wave

". . . what can you do with the love you feel? Where is there you can take it?"

—From *Picnic*

"The success racket consumes and wastes talent mercilessly," observes Harold Clurman in *Lies Like Truth*.[1] Everyone knows that "if at first you don't succeed [you must] try, try again," but no comparable bit of doggerel tells people what to do once they succeed, because then they have set a standard for themselves to be measured against. This specter can be intimidating to even the stoutest of heart. When one's success is literary, it often deprives authors of the privacy and solitude that writing requires.

The early recognition that *Come Back, Little Sheba* brought William Inge left him first bewildered, then depressed, a reaction similar to what Tennessee Williams felt after *The Glass Menagerie* had taken audiences by storm.[2] Inge had always dreamed of success, but it seemed elusive and unreal, something that awaited him in some far-off future. When that murky future metamorphosed into the present, Inge was amazed at his reaction to success. He had expected to feel hilarious but, instead, found himself in a depressive funk.[3] Certainly during the rehearsals of *Sheba*, he learned some hard lessons about the playwright's role in the production of his own plays.

The outstanding commercial and artistic success of the three plays that followed *Sheba—Picnic, Bus Stop,* and *The Dark at the Top of the Stairs*—amazed critics and the public alike. Inge had cause for elation but lived rather with a festering insecurity that he sought to overcome with alcohol and tranquilizers. He experienced the kind of torment that led him in 1967 to tell Digby Diehl, "I think that the instant a person becomes famous in America[,] a machine is set in motion to destroy him. If you look at the personal lives of people in the theater in this country[,] most of them are despairingly unhappy people. We have no future and security to offer them."[4] Even when he was riding the crest of his wave of popularity and acceptance in 1958, Inge wrote that none of his plays had brought him the kind of joy he had craved and anticipated.[5] He soon learned that success does not mean that one has won the game; it means instead that the stakes are higher, the competition fiercer.

All four plays of Inge's most successful period pose the question of what love means in modern society. They are concerned even more, however, with questions of personal isolation, both physical and spiritual. The characters in each of these plays are hindered in their attempts to find identity in the situations in which Inge places them. They all have difficulty communicating on any but a superficial level—a common problem among twentieth-century Americans. Most of the characters in Inge's four major plays have never come to grips with themselves, have never really understood their own beings. Most of them serve time toward some undefined end. They live out the days and weeks of their lives engaged in commonplace, monotonous activities, facing with resignation the tedium that constitutes their lives.

At the end of each of these plays, Inge suggests that a resolution has been reached. Lola reconciles with Doc in the closing minutes of *Sheba,* accepting him as he is, not as she would prefer him to be. Madge, in one version of *Picnic,* follows Hal, while in another version, she reverts to the life she has been living, presumably better able to accept it because of the interval that Hal provided her. Cherie in *Bus Stop* consents to marry Bo. She goes to Montana with him, seemingly to live happily ever after, although one must question whether Inge's solution is tenable. In *Dark,* Cora follows Rubin upstairs, to where there is a spot of light, suggesting that their marriage will now enter a more fulfilling stage than was previously possible. One wonders, however, whether Cora's frigidity can be overcome quite so easily as Inge suggests.

In each case, nothing much changes. The audience is left with the inevitable suspicion that the solutions Inge has found to his characters' problems will not work for long. The resolutions in each case are symptomatic of the spiritual and emotional bankruptcy of the characters Inge portrays. Is their acceptance of their lots not the greatest defeat of all? Does this sort of compromise not represent resolution by default rather than resolution by design?

Inge's first four Broadway productions are intensely realistic. Willard Thorpe wrote, "The realism of [Inge's] plots and dialogue suggests the kinds of dramas with which the playwrights of the early 1920s broke the earlier tradition of sentimentality and melodrama in the theatre."[6] Inge's realism stems from his awareness that there is a great deal of fraud and hypocrisy in human behavior, particularly in human sexuality. He once observed that from childhood he was always curious that the women he knew as he was growing up in Kansas protested while the men pursued, suggesting that women hated men. He finally realized, however, that there was an artificiality in this scenario, that some women are embarrassed by the extent of their love and passion, which makes them dependent on men.[7] The male–female relationships in Inge's plays and novels reflect exactly the sentiment the author expressed in this interview.

Inge's presentation of male–female relationships provides the key to understanding his essential realism. He shows bare human sexual motivation and, like Williams, Arthur Miller, and Carson McCullers, brings one face to face with the compromises a passive—or sometimes malevolent—society forces upon people.

Come Back, Little Sheba

Many people consider *Come Back, Little Sheba* Inge's best play.[8] It has greater structural unity and a stronger story line than any of his other plays, with the possible exception of his scenario, *Splendor in the Grass*. Much of what has been written about *Sheba* has not noted the care with which Inge brought unity to his script.

Sheba is largely a story of contrasts, a presentation of thesis and antithesis. If any synthesis occurs, it is found in the resignation with which the two major characters, Doc and Lola, face the prospect of going on pretty much as they always have. No positive forces lead them to the conclusion that they will be better off spending the rest of their lives together. Lola has no choice. She has tried to escape from her situation by telephoning her mother to tell her how unhappy she is and to ask if her father might not let her come home for a little while, but her mother discourages her from doing so. Doc, just having returned home from the drunk tank at City Hospital, begs Lola not to leave him because, if she does, he might have to spend the rest of his life in the drunk tank.

Lola and Doc have both had their decisions made for them. Lola, thirty-eight years old, uncaring about her appearance, untrained, and without work experience, has no place to go, no way to support herself, if she leaves Doc. Doc, a chiropractor able to support both of them in the sexist world in which the play takes place, looks to Lola as his only means of evading the terror of the drunk tank. Presumably the two will stay together for the rest of their lives because they have no alternative. They will not endure because they really want to, but rather because they can deal with each other's weaknesses.

Sheba is a tale of personal failure and frustration, and of the attendant loneliness that is inevitable for the two central characters, Lola and Doc, who have been married for twenty years. The garrulous Lola, based on a sister of Inge's mother,[9] reveals the past in reminiscences with Doc. She was overly protected by a suspicious father who approved of none of her suitors until Doc, then a premedical student, began to court her. Doc apparently was a fine figure of a man, a far cry from the dissipated wreck the audience sees in the play. Doc courted Lola, a high school beauty queen, for a year before he got up the nerve to kiss her. When the first kiss finally came, the emotional pitch of the experience caused tears to well up in Doc's eyes.

Having overcome his basic reticence, Doc apparently proceeded with great dispatch to get Lola pregnant and to marry her under duress. Lola miscarried, apparently because the midwife, to whom Lola resorted because she felt too guilty to go to a regular obstetrician, botched the delivery. Lola was unable to have other children.

Through Lola's talkathons with anyone willing to listen—her roomer, Marie; Marie's boyfriend, Turk; the postman; the milkman; the next-door neighbor—the audience is told in considerable detail of Doc's alcoholism and of what he is doing to overcome it, of Doc's refusal to let Lola take a job when they were first married, of how Lola's father reacted to her pregnancy, and of the other necessary business of the drama. Inge's Lola is a one-woman chorus. Although the device is somewhat contrived and occasionally tiresome, it works as a means for Inge to present necessary details efficiently in a short space. Lola's logorrhea also highlights her loneliness and frustration. She will talk to anyone, but no one wants to listen. The device also heightens the monotony of the first part of the play to such an extent that the ultimate clash between Lola and Doc has the effect of a tidal wave of action and emotional intensity.

Most of *Sheba's* critics consider the slow buildup to the drunk scene a technical flaw. They feel that the drunk scene surges with vitality, but that it has been too long in coming. Inge's design in delaying the crucial action, however, was well calculated. He consciously constructed his play this way so that it would resemble the force of a tornado, which begins with a frightening quiet followed by unbelievable violence.[10]

The drunk scene itself consumed seventeen minutes in the New York staging of the play as Daniel Mann directed it. Mann capitalized on the violence of this scene, and Sidney Blackmer (Doc) was injured several times as he threw himself into his performance. Blackmer said, however, that this climactic scene was "easier to play than the scenes of restraint and repression that lead up to it and which, by contrast, make the explosive scene so expressive."[11] The sudden action of the drunk scene provides the most notable structural contrast in a play whose content is largely dependent on constant contrasts.

Among these contrasts is that between Lola and her roomer, Marie, an art student with a realistic outlook and the morals of a cat. Lola, once beautiful like Marie, is now overweight, sloppy, and shiftless. Marie plans to marry her socially prominent, well-fixed suitor, Bruce. Bruce, however, lives in Cincinnati, some distance from where Marie goes to school, so she carries on an affair with Turk, a brainless hunk of flesh who throws the javelin. The night before Bruce is to arrive for a visit, Turk stays over with Marie. When Lola asks Marie if Turk will feel badly about Bruce's coming to visit, Marie tells her that it will bother him for a while, but that he has his eye on a Spanish girl in one of his classes. Inge wrote *Sheba* at a time when Marie's statement was an early harbinger of the new morality that swept the country in the next decade.

One of Lola's few pleasures in life is living the vicarious experiences she has through Marie. In Lola's stalwart approval of Turk and in her complete acceptance of Marie's affair with him are found both the basis for much of the conflict between Doc and Lola and an indication that Lola, who was forced into an early marriage before she had experienced sex with anyone except Doc, has always hankered for the kind of sheer animal pleasure that a brute like Turk provides.

Lola's last dream involves Turk's throwing of his highly Freudian javelin. It reinforces the basic phallic fascination Turk holds for Lola. Turk, of course, holds the same fascination for Marie, who might, given twenty more years, turn out like Lola. Turk is Inge's attempt to present the Stanley Kowalski type that Williams popularized in *A Streetcar*

Named Desire. Long on bulging biceps and short on brains, the T-shirt is his emblem. He is all animal, and he flutters female pulses by his overwhelming sexuality. Awkward in anything smaller than a stadium, he is gauche and crude, destructive yet commanding, the quality that makes him irresistible.

In the figure of the milkman, Inge provides another sketch of the muscleman, but one less fully realized than Turk. In both of these portrayals, however, Inge moves toward presenting the kind of male animal he uses to advance the action of both *Picnic* and *Good Luck, Miss Wyckoff.* In both cases, the motivating force behind the action is a sexually disturbing male.

Lola, who has been monogamous, feels cheated that she has not known anyone sexually except Doc. She cannot acknowledge this feeling to herself, however, because of the puritanical standards by which she was raised. Although they live under the same roof, Lola and Doc have been separated from each other through the years because they are unable to communicate. They do not know each other well enough even to be angry with each other. They are polite in the way that two people are who have just met. Their aggressions smoulder under a facade of indifference, resignation, and apathy—except when Doc is drunk.

When Doc corrects Lola, who has made a coarse utterance, her response is lifeless. When Lola uses the word "pooped," Doc admonishes her, tells her the word is vulgar. Lola says she heard Marie and Turk use it and thought it was cute, but promises not to use it again. In this exchange, as in several others, she tellingly calls Doc "Daddy." The amiability the speech reflects can be attributed only to apathy.

A further example of this avoidance of unpleasantness, of confrontation, occurs when Lola makes no secret of having steamed open Bruce's telegram to Marie and read it. Doc tells Lola that nice people don't do things like that. Lola shows her utter lack of ethical sensitivity in matters of this sort by responding somewhat uncomprehendingly, that she doesn't see any harm in what she has done, especially because she has resealed the telegram so that Marie will never know it. Doc just shrugs indifferently and dismisses the matter, calling Lola "Baby," and saying that if she doesn't realize what is wrong with what she has done, he guesses he can't make her understand her transgression. Clearly after twenty years of living together, Doc and Lola share virtually no common values, and both retreat from the possibility of establishing any.

Lola's next-door neighbor, Mrs. Coffman, contrasts sharply to the slatternly Lola. Mrs. Coffman, mother of seven, does not have Lola's easy life. She has no time to sit around and chat. Just as Marie's beauty is juxtaposed to Lola's unattractiveness, so the busy, family-oriented Mrs. Coffman's hard work and organization are in sharp contrast to Lola's laziness and lack of organization. The contrast is intensified when Mrs. Coffman's fertility is juxtaposed to Lola's barrenness. Just before Mrs. Coffman exits from her first brief appearance in the play, she tells Lola with some annoyance and with a sense of superiority that she cannot have coffee and chat with her because she has work to do.

Inge makes it clear, also, that Mrs. Coffman commands more respect than Lola does because when the milkman enters just before Mrs. Coffman's exit, he greets her by name. But when Lola greets the milkman pleasantly, he just calls her "Lady." Lola's rejection by both Mrs. Coffman and the milkman reinforces Inge's representation of what Lola's life is. Her husband seemingly rejects her as a wife, and her father rejects her as a daughter because she became pregnant out of wedlock. Although Turk and Marie tolerate Lola, Turk does not mask his annoyance at her constant presence. Marie reacts to Lola out of pity rather than out of fondness or respect.

Lola's life is out of control. She looks back on twenty years of marriage and has nothing to show for it. Her most notable achievement has been in keeping Doc away from the bottle, but the play does not contain a single line to suggest even remotely that Lola has ever in all her thirty-eight years experienced anything that faintly resembles fulfillment. She is too emotionally immature to have a stable relationship of any kind with another human being. She finds herself, in W. H. Auden's words, "Alone and afraid / In a world I never made."

Inge implies in *Sheba,* as in much of his other work, the loneliness and fear inherent in the human condition. The best one can expect in life is the sort of compromise, the sort of bleak interdependency that Doc and Lola settle for to keep from being completely alone. After twenty years together, each has robbed the other of any chance to find a satisfactory human relationship. A fear that borders on hysteria becomes the single bond that unites them. Each is in the sort of trap T. S. Eliot presents toward the end of *The Cocktail Party,* when Edward and his wife, Lavinia, upper-crust versions of Doc and Lola, simply resign themselves to making the best of a hopeless situation.

The dynamics of the Doc/Lola/Marie relationship show Inge in excellent control of dramatic situation. Lola muses to Doc that if they had had the baby, she would be a young woman by now. Doc might have saved his money rather than drinking it away so that their child could go to college like Marie, who is obviously a surrogate daughter for both Doc and Lola. But Marie is more as well: to Lola, she is a major means of vicarious fulfillment, while to Doc, she represents what might have been. Doc, who is in love with Marie, is afraid to admit his feelings even to himself. In his twisted emotional state about her, he becomes virtually obsessed with the illusion of her purity. Predictably, Doc treats Turk hatefully because Turk threatens the illusion of Marie's purity, and this illusion is essential to Doc's emotional equilibrium.

Doc's hatred of Turk precipitates the basic conflict between Doc and Lola. Doc is annoyed that Lola encourages the Marie–Turk affair and is utterly appalled when she actually promotes it by welcoming Turk into the house and by leaving Marie alone with him in the evening. The one time Doc rises above his apathy without the stimulation of alcohol occurs when he complains to Lola because she permits Turk to pose for Marie in his track suit. Lola's explanation that Marie is just having him pose for a picture she is drawing does not assuage Doc's anger, and as the curtain falls, Doc shouts that he will never forgive Lola if anything happens to Marie.

Inge leaves little doubt that Doc's love for Marie is more than fatherly. Early in the play,[12] Doc picks up Marie's scarf and looks at it fondly. This action recurs (77) when Doc picks up Marie's scarf and fondles it in act 2. Doc's Madonna image of Marie becomes clear when he turns on the radio and, according to Inge's directions, tunes in to a rendition of Shubert's *Ave Maria* sung in a high soprano voice. He listens intently.

Lola intrudes upon his reverie, slamming the back door and announcing that she is "pooped." Doc's mood is shattered. Inge uses a similar idea in the scene where Doc is fondling Marie's scarf. The sound of Turk's laughter reaches him from Marie's bedroom, and the directions indicate that the laughter, like that of a sated Bacchus, shatters Doc's reverie (77).

Shortly after this episode, Doc takes a bottle from its hiding place and breaks his hard-won abstinence. Inge purposefully has Doc's single eruption of temper while he is sober occur just after he has fondled Marie's scarf for the first time. After he had fondled the scarf for the second time, Turk's bacchanalian laughter intrudes upon his reverie. Doc now yields to the temptation he has resisted for several years, setting the stage for the sequence of events that leads up to his violent drunk scene, the most crucial action in the play.

Inge uses Marie as an unwitting triggering device. She is not aware that Doc is jealous of Turk, even though Turks tells her that such is the case (66). But Doc never shows his jealousy overtly, nor does he reveal his jealousy of Turk in Marie's presence. When Lola suggests that Doc speak to Marie if he thinks Turk should not pose for her in skimpy attire, Doc demurs (41).

Nevertheless, Marie has created the situation about which Doc and Lola disagree, and it is this situation that causes Doc to start drinking. If there is any hope at the end of the play, it is that Doc returns home chastened by his harrowing experience in City Hospital. Marie by now has eloped with Bruce. Perhaps with Marie gone, Doc and Lola will regain their balance, but it seems unlikely that they will ever find their real identities or that they will ever understand themselves or each other.

In *Sheba,* Lola is more fully realized than Doc. In all his work, Inge had a fine ability to write about the female mentality, which he understood much better and much more instinctively than he did the male. In *Sheba,* the audience is told what Doc might have been. Doc himself reiterates the promise of his youth, speculating on how he might have been a successful medical doctor instead of what he is (56). But one must at this point question whether Doc ever had the potential of which he speaks.

Inge, of course, might have been trying to indicate how completely Lola has drained Doc of every vestige of the promise he showed as a young man. But as Doc appears in *Sheba,* he is so lacking in drive that one must question whether he ever had the sort of initiative it would take for him to be a "big M. D.," as he calls it. It seems more likely that Doc has found his level and that he has achieved his best or very close to it. Is it not possible that he has clung to Lola through the years because he can use her as the visible explanation for his lack of success? Perhaps he needs Lola as his rationalization to the world for not having fulfilled the mythical potential he liked to think he had.

The drunk scene provides a telling insight into what Doc really feels. In it, all of Doc's inhibitions about Lola—but not his inhibitions about Marie—are off. Doc's unacknowledged love for Marie is obviously the most important motivating factor in this agonizingly tense scene. The surface motivation for the drunk scene is Doc's anger at Lola because she has quite uncharacteristically cleaned the house and prepared a good meal for Marie's boyfriend, Bruce. However, the real reason for the scene is that Doc's desire for and jealousy of Marie have reached the crisis stage and are overpowering him. Even in his drunken state, Doc must repress his true feelings for Marie, but he reveals them obliquely, first by scolding Lola for not even sweeping the floors until "some bozo" comes to romance Marie (96), and then by flourishing a hatchet and railing that he should hack Lola's fat off, chop off Marie's ankles, and "fix" Turk (97).

It is significant that Doc does not propose killing Marie but rather mutilating her in such a way that she will be unable ever to walk away from him. His desire to mutilate the loved one—whom he cannot have as she now is—is sound psychologically. In a sense, Doc is in a situation comparable to Ethan Frome's. In *Ethan Frome,* mutilation occurs when death was intended, and the bitterness of Ethan's unrequited love is made all the more poignant as Mattie Silver grows into a hag with a much sharper tongue than Zeena ever had.

Doc's language also implies that he does not want to kill Turk, but rather that he wants to castrate him, to rob him of his pervasive sexuality. Inge chooses the word "fix" calculatedly, bearing in mind its full connotation.

Doc's idea of purity is tied up with his veneration for his mother, and this is one reason that he cannot face his own feelings toward Marie, whom he has, in his own mind, turned into a Madonna. Doc suffers from deep-seated Oedipus problems that make his feelings toward Marie unbearable for him. When he pulls the cloth off the table Lola has set with her best Haviland dishes, a wedding gift from Doc's mother, and sends the dishes crashing to the floor, he shouts at Lola that his mother didn't give them these dishes so that whores could eat from them (96).

One of *Sheba's* most successful contrasts occurs when Doc has been taken to City Hospital to dry out in its drunk tank and Lola is left home alone. No sooner has Doc left than Marie and Bruce, ignorant of what has just happened, arrive. Because they have been out all night, they know nothing of the events that Marie has innocently precipitated. When the young couple comes into the room, Marie tells Lola to congratulate her because she and Bruce are to be married (107). She is going to quit school and go away with him at once.

The timing in this scene is dramatically superb. Lola, with Doc in the drunk tank and Marie about to leave, realizes how totally alone she is. She telephones to her mother only to be rebuffed because the mother knows that Lola's father will not allow Lola in his house. Her isolation and loneliness at this point are complete. As the curtain falls on act 2, scene 3, the pervading sense of depression is total. All hope appears to be gone, yet it is from this situation that Lola must go on. Marie's telling Lola to congratulate her as she comes bounding on the scene with Bruce in tow is wholly ironic and emphasizes the lack of communication Marie has with Lola. Marie has room only for her own happiness.

Sheba's symbolism, much of it contained in Lola's dreams, is pervasive and often obvious. The New York critics subjected the dreams in the play to harsh criticism even though Inge had several psychiatrists read the play before its production, and they had no significant quarrel with the dream sequences on psychological grounds. Inge countered the criticism of the dreams by pointing out their dramatic function, whether they were scientifically sound or not.[13]

The first dream Lola reveals to the audience is her recurrent one about the loss of her little dog, Sheba. In this dream, it is soon apparent that Sheba is the symbolic representation of Lola's lost youth, and the loss of the dog is synonymous with the passing of her youth. Lola dreams that she puts Sheba on a leash and takes her downtown, where everyone on the street turns to admire the dog, which makes Lola proud (7). Lola, as a beauty queen, was much admired in her own youth.

Lola continues, telling of how, all at once, Sheba, who couldn't keep up with her, is nowhere to be found. Lola, fearful, refuses to believe the loss is permanent. She asks Doc if he thinks that means that Sheba is gone for good. Doc can only say that Sheba should have stayed young forever (8). The irony here is that Lola, whom Sheba represents, is growing old but remains immature.

In three separate instances, Lola indicates her sense of loss. She talks with Doc about Sheba, telling him that she just "vanished into thin air" (9). Later, as she reminisces with Doc about their courtship, she begins to think of the twenty years that have passed and have robbed her of her youth, and she uses the same terminology she used in talking about Sheba's disappearance. Like Sheba, Lola's last twenty years, her youth, have "vanished into thin air" (53).

The last occurrence of this terminology occurs when Lola has prepared dinner for Bruce and Marie. She has decorated with flowers. She comments on how lovely the flowers are, but goes on to say that they, like Sheba and her youth, will not last long. After a few days they, too, will "vanish into thin air" (85). But this time Lola is in a much happier mood than she was when she spoke similar words earlier. She takes a spare flower and gives it to Marie to put in her hair, perhaps suggesting that Lola is beginning to gain a perspective, however slight, on her situation.

Another pervasive and telling symbol that appears along with Sheba in Lola's final dream (117–18) is the symbol of the javelin. Turk, whose sexuality is emphasized throughout the play, is in training for spring track. He tells Lola early in the play that he throws the javelin. Lola doesn't know what a javelin is, and Turk tells her that it is a long lance that one holds erect. He then tells how he lets it go so that it flies through the air until it lands in the ground yards away and quivers (22). The sexual connotations are overpowering, but lest the audience have any doubt, Inge later reiterates the meaning of this symbol in preparation for the meaning he intends it to have in the final dream sequence, upon which the suggested solution to Doc and Lola's problems depends. Turk propositions Marie, who coyly reminds Turk he is in training. His reply, rich in double entendres, is that he can throw that old javelin any old time (70).

In the closing minutes of the play, Doc says that he might take up hunting and get a bird dog, which would, of course, replace the missing Sheba. Then Lola tells him of her final dream that takes her back to a scene from her youth, to her high school, where she and Marie are going to the Olympics. She makes a point of saying that thousands of people were there and that Turk was out in the field throwing the javelin. It is clear from the fact that thousands are watching that Lola is trying to assuage her guilt feelings about having eavesdropped on Marie and Turk at various stages of their lovemaking throughout the play, an aberration for which Doc has scolded her.

In Lola's dream, her father is in charge of the games. Turk keeps changing into someone else as the dream progresses. Lola's father finally disqualifies Turk just as he had disqualified all of Lola's would-be suitors. Doc replaces Turk on the field, and Lola's dream brings from her subconscious the memory of what Doc used to be to her. In her dream he picks up the javelin carefully, not impetuously as Turk had, and throws it so high into the air that it doesn't come down (118). As rain begins to fall, Lola misses Sheba. She searches in the crowd for her and all at once sees her dead in the middle of the field. In Lola's dream, Sheba's white (virginal) fur is smeared with mud (loss of innocence) and no one stops to take care of the dead dog (parental rejection) (118).

The play closes with small indications that Lola is perhaps ready to face life on more realistic terms than she previously had. She has made a start by filling out the dairy order slip rather than waiting for the milkman so that she can trap him into conversation. She finally tells Doc that she has given up hope that Sheba will come back, and she decides not to call her any more (119).

Inge thought of *Sheba* as a "pathetic comedy." Certainly it is not a tragedy in either the classical or modern sense of tragedy, partly at least because the real tragedy took place long before the play opened and what is about to happen is not tragic by comparison. If Doc's not becoming an M.D. represents the fall of a protagonist, the fall took place too long before the action of the play to have direct bearing on the play itself.

At best the play is melancholic rather than tragic. The theme of continuance is strong and is reinforced by one of Doc's speeches, in which he says that it is necessary to keep living, not to give up because of a few mistakes (56). One is left with the feeling that Doc and Lola will persist now that Marie is out of their lives. Perhaps they will learn from what they have suffered. More probably, however, their lives will not be much different from what they have been up until now.

The initial critical opinion of *Sheba* was somewhat divided,[14] but the play was generally well thought of and could probably have had a longer run had it not been necessary for Shirley Booth and Sidney Blackmer to leave their roles in order to honor other commitments. *Sheba* was well received on tour[15] and has been revived regularly since its first production.

Picnic and *Summer Brave*

Picnic[16] takes place on Labor Day, but it might as easily have taken place on May Day because, as Joshua Logan staged it, the central figure, Hal Carter, is the quintessence of sexuality and, like the May pole, stands as a great phallic presence in the midst of a bevy of confused, bored, sexually frustrated women who dance around him. However, Inge selects Labor Day because it heralds the end of summer, which in the play signifies the end of youth. Labor Day has special meaning for Rosemary Sydney, the spinster schoolteacher who boards with the Owens family. This is her last day of summer before school begins, but it is also virtually her last chance to find love before her youth has faded totally. Like Miss Wyckoff in Inge's later novel, Rosemary has led a life of moral restraint and sexual frustration, not unlike that Inge himself experienced when he taught in small midwestern towns.[17]

Rosemary loathes returning to the dull repetition of another year of teaching, of having her evening meal with other spinster teachers, then coming home alone (*P*, 130). She tells her boyfriend Howard that every year she tells herself this is her last year of teaching, that something will happen to take her away from it. And every year, she admits, she gets a little crazier (*P*, 130). Every character in the play suffers from the same basic insecurity that makes Rosemary reach out pitifully toward Howard—not because she loves him, but because she fears she will continue to live this life until she is ready for the cemetery and has no one to take her there (*P*, 129).

Picnic, the basis of which is *Front Porch*, a fragmentary play that Inge wrote shortly after *Farther Off from Heaven*, consisted initially of little more than character sketches of five women living humdrum existences in a small Kansas town. Inge wrote, "I was fascinated to find how . . . the women seemed to have created a world of their own, a world in which they seemed to be pretending men did not exist. It was a world that had to be destroyed, at least for dramatic values."[18] Inge created a female microcosm, into which he introduced Hal Carter. The play deals with the unsettling effect Hal's presence has on the women and on the society of which they are a part.

As the play was originally conceived, it had no main character. Inge was not eager at first to impose a story upon his sketches of five frustrated women.[19] Then he realized that something had to happen to disturb his five characters. He struck on the idea of introducing a handsome male stripped to the waist and surging with a sexuality that would throw his characters into a state of emotional chaos.

In Hal, Inge created a composite figure who has the athletic ability and erotic appeal of Turk in *Sheba* and of Rafe in *Good Luck, Miss Wyckoff*, but who also has the insecurity problems and the dependence of a character like Doc Delaney. Inge gives Hal trappings of a surface virility—a dirty T-shirt, blue jeans, cowboy boots, and a great hairy chest that holds immense fascination for the women in the play, even though Flo Owens and Rosemary make a point of objecting heartily to Hal's working around Helen Potts's yard with his T-shirt off.

When audiences disliked Hal in out-of-town tryouts of the play,[20] Inge gave him all the excuses he could for having the overpowering sense of inferiority and insecurity that he shows and that sometimes manifests itself in obnoxious behavior. Hal has spent a year in a reformatory because his mother did not care enough about him to save him from this fate when she could have, just as Donnie Barker's mother, Sue, in *Natural Affection* would not adjust her life so that Donnie could live with her rather than remain in the reformatory. Hal's fraternity brothers rejected him because of his crude manners. He has been forced to leave college for academic inadequacy. His father, with whom he had a degree of rapport, dies after being jailed for public drunkenness. Hal's only friend, Alan Seymour, is not very fond of Hal.

In an unpublished master's thesis on Inge, Jerry L. Crawford says, "the organizational core [of *Picnic*] is in the use of character. . . . The dramatic progression of *Picnic* is controlled by character through the beginning, middle, and end action." Crawford goes on, "In all three organizational units Inge causes the spectator to be concerned primarily with the development of character, not with what is going to happen in the action."[21] In this respect, *Picnic* is drastically different from *Sheba*, in which the characterization, although strong, is governed by the play's rising action.

Picnic begins with immediate conflict in a minor key, as Millie, Madge Owens's sixteen-year-old sister, is seen sitting on the back stoop clandestinely smoking a forbidden cigarette. The newspaper boy comes by and serves an important function in antagonizing Millie and making it obvious that she feels like an ugly duckling, as well as in eliciting comments from Millie that make clear her feelings of jealousy toward the beautiful Madge. Millie, knowing that she can never be like Madge, has never tried, adopting instead a tomboy demeanor. The newsboy also prepares the audience for Madge's appearance by commenting on her great beauty. The rivalry, resentment, and contention between the two sisters surface immediately. Each envies what the other has. Millie envies Madge's good looks; Madge envies Millie's intelligence.

Hal has already appeared on stage when Madge makes her first entrance. He has been seen working around Helen Potts's yard and has been described as a handsome vagabond.[22] In an early exchange between Madge and the newsboy, Bomber, it is revealed that because Madge is planning to marry Alan Seymour, the son of well-to-do local banker, she cannot date other boys. Hal is brought into the action when he chivalrously comes to Madge's defense after Bomber grabs her arm. He sends Bomber scurrying and, his face lighting up, greets Madge. She responds, and the two look self-consciously at each other (*P*, 78). The animal magnetism that attracts them is immediately apparent in this meeting. Before the play is five minutes old, the inevitable outcome is perfectly clear.

Hal and Madge are alike in a number of ways. Hal is handsome, Madge is beautiful. Each has been stumbling through life trying to find security. Hal has sought to find himself first by going to college on an athletic scholarship—only to fail—and then by trying unsuccessfully to break into films. His goals have proved unrealistic. Now, disillusioned, he wants to settle down somewhere. Society has rejected him so often that, despite his displays of braggadocio, he lacks self-confidence. Madge, on the surface at least, has had an easier life than Hal. She appears to have the quiet confidence that sometimes goes with great beauty, and Alan Seymour, a most eligible bachelor, is worshipfully in love with her.

Nevertheless, Madge's security is skin-deep. Her insecurities begin to surface when she confesses to her mother that she is uncomfortable around Alan's friends (*P*, 81) because they have been to college and have traveled in Europe. Madge thinks she is not their equal. She feels out of place in the company of those who have had advantages she has not had. Madge also suffers from the "Marilyn Monroe problem"— she fears people appreciate her only for her beauty and asks her mother what good it is to be pretty. She complains that she is tired of being looked at, that she sees no value in being pretty (*P*, 84). The audience senses Madge's double conflict, which is heightened through the first act, in which it is obvious that Alan Seymour values Madge for her beauty, looking upon her as a beautiful *object,* a showpiece to be admired when his friends see him with her.

It is also revealed that Alan's refinement exceeds his virility. In an awkward scene between Flo and Madge, Flo asks if Alan ever wants to go beyond kissing when they are together. Madge, much embarrassed by her mother's question, admits that he does. When Flo asks Madge whether it upsets Alan to be refused, Madge tells her that it doesn't, that Alan is not like most boys (*P*, 80). The Hal–Alan situation is much like the Turk–Bruce situation in *Sheba.*

The first act of *Picnic* is technically interesting because the rising action develops in two separate lines, one for Hal, another for Madge. This heterodox dramatic procedure has evoked some adverse comment from critics who failed to realize what the author was attempting to achieve. Hal and Madge are both engaged in a conflict against society. As the two parts of the rising action progress, they move closer and closer together until they merge into a single line.

Inge permitted the two lines of development to remain merged in the Broadway production of *Picnic*. In *Summer Brave*, however, the lines separate in the falling action. Hal goes to Tulsa, and Madge, having lost both Alan and Hal, returns to her dead-end job at the five-and-dime. In both versions, Hal has served the purpose of making Madge realize that she will not find fulfillment in life if she goes after the materialistic sort of security that her mother wants for her.

Madge's mother, Flo Owens, has an immediate and instinctive fear of Hal. She recognizes in him the same animal attractiveness to which she succumbed as a girl. Her life has been difficult and unhappy because she married a handsome, lovable, irresponsible stud who left her with two children and no forwarding address. Flo's first unpleasant encounter with Hal results in her asking him to get off her property. It is ironic, then, that she is finally forced to accept Hal because of her admiration for Alan Seymour and that she has to accede to Hal's coming to the Labor Day picnic with them. When she discovers that Hal and Alan are old friends, she grudgingly accepts him (*P,* 96). Inge has effectively removed the major obstacle, a suspicious and objecting mother, from the Madge–Hal scene.

The credit for discovering Hal must go to Helen Potts, the next-door neighbor, an incurable romantic who insists on calling herself "Mrs." even though her marriage to a young man was never consummated and was over within days of the wedding when her possessive, demanding mother obtained an annulment for her. Helen, whose young man was subsequently killed in the war, is now almost totally consumed by her clutching mother, old and ill. Helen's only outward rebellion against the older woman is to call herself "Mrs." Helen basically is a good person. Although she has ample cause to be bitter, she does not show evidence of a real, festering bitterness. Rather, she is outgoing and sincere. She grasps the opportunity to bring Hal into her house because he represents all that she has missed in life.

Certainly Helen Potts has no hope of attracting Hal herself, even though she would like to. Like Lola in *Sheba,* she has to settle for watching his developing relationship with Madge. Romantic though she is, Mrs. Potts is capable of facing and accepting life's stark realities. This quality is especially evident when Madge and Hal start to dance together in what Inge identifies as a primitive rite, while everyone watches. Mrs. Potts gazes in fascination, then, indeed quite generously, remarks that the two seem to be made for each other (*P*, 120).

Rosemary Sydney, the schoolteacher, also watches this dance. Already stimulated by having taken an unaccustomed swig of whiskey from Howard's bottle, the primitive sexuality inherent in the dance makes her realize her own frustration, which rises up so unbearably that she must vent it somehow. She needs a scapegoat. First she rants at Howard because he can't dance like that, then she throws herself at Hal in such an obvious way that he, mightily embarrassed, is forced to retreat, in essence to reject Rosemary's advances. This action precipitates Rosemary's violent verbal attack upon Hal, and this unfair and uncalled-for attack arouses Madge's (and the audience's) sympathy for Hal and precipitates the Hal–Madge affair.

Hal's presence results directly in Rosemary's compromising Howard, a poor dupe who has no idea that an hour or two in the moonlight with Rosemary will result in his having to marry her. Rosemary is a fully realized and excellently portrayed dramatic character. One might question the advisability of relegating her to a secondary plot in *Picnic* because Rosemary seems well enough realized to deserve a central role.

In *Picnic*, Rosemary and Millie are closely akin dramatically. Both pretend a disinclination toward men because each is afraid of rejection and is put on the defensive by her growing fear and insecurity. Millie finds sublimation in her reading and in her daydreams of becoming a novelist who will shock readers (*P*, 146). But for Rosemary no such sublimation is feasible. Despite all her talk to the contrary, Rosemary is going to claim her man. She spends hours working on her face and hair. She dresses with great care. In *Summer Brave*, Inge makes a point of having Flo comment on all her preparations and proclaim that Rosemary is indeed out to get her man (*SB*, 35).

Rosemary seethes with an inner tumult quite common to people in her situation at her age, particularly before the era of women's rights and sexual liberation. She is preoccupied with sex, something she cannot admit to any of the people around her and something that she cannot show in any overt actions without the risk of being ostracized by those who control her life as a schoolteacher in a small Kansas town, ironically called Liberty. She is in the same sort of situation that Miss Wyckoff is in *Good Luck, Miss Wyckoff*, a bright, sensitive woman who, in her mid-thirties, still rents a room in someone else's house and who takes her dinners in a local restaurant with people much like herself.

Worse even than her present situation is the fact that she has thirty more years to teach, thirty more years to live this futile existence, before she can hope for something else—unless she marries. She is faced with choosing between two quite bleak alternatives: to teach for thirty more years or to marry someone she does not love and at least have her own home to live in and someone to share life with.

Painfully aware that she is aging, Rosemary is more at sea than Hal even though she has more material security than he. By developing a rigid personality, Rosemary has been able to make a half-hearted adjustment to her life. When Hal comes on the scene, her equilibrium and fragile personality are shattered. In *Summer Brave* the audience first sees Rosemary on the porch dressed in an old kimono, her hair half set, her face covered with cold cream.

Her first line is a rationalization to the effect that in a small town like Liberty, she can go around looking however she pleases on a September morning (*SB,* 18). She quickly negates this sentiment, however, when, within a few speeches, she agrees with her landlady, Flo, that Helen Potts should make Hal put on his shirt when he is working around the yard. The sight of his bare flesh and hairy chest is more than Rosemary can cope with, and is something that Helen Potts is unwilling to deal with.

Rosemary will probably be a better person for having yielded to her passion, thereby overcoming a few of the crippling inhibitions she has been struggling against. Her passion, of course, is for Hal; Howard is the best surrogate available to her, so she leads him on, then coyly yields to him. The real clue to Rosemary's salvation comes when, quite uncharacteristically, she begs Howard to marry her. In doing so, she demonstrates that her brave, independent pose is nothing but a pose. In *Picnic,* Howard exits without saying whether he will accept Rosemary's proposal that they marry. As he exits, a completely humbled, supplicating Rosemary begs him to marry her.

In this version of the play, Howard returns the next morning, probably to tell Rosemary he will not marry her. He does not get to see her alone, however, because two other teachers are with her when he arrives. The implication is that Rosemary, before two witnesses, will trap him into saying that he will marry her, and that she will probably spend the rest of her life with him, living the kind of compromise that Lola does with Doc and that Cora does with Rubin.

In *Summer Brave,* however, Howard accepts Rosemary's proposal before he exits—but not until she has humbled herself and begged him to marry her, indicating that some of the steel has gone out of her soul, that she is becoming more human. *Picnic*'s ending is stronger than *Summer Brave*'s because in it Rosemary is permitted to retain at least a shred of her dignity, and the audience is forced to decide what the outcome will be.

Technically, *Picnic* is an admirable play. If anything in it is out of focus, it is that the secondary plot is so strong that it provides formidable competition to the play's major plot. It is, indeed, a sufficiently strong plot to have warranted full treatment itself as a separate work, which essentially happened with *Good Luck, Miss Wyckoff*.

Rosemary remains one of Inge's memorable portrayals, even more successful than her counterpart in *Good Luck, Miss Wyckoff*, because in the novel readers are told more about Miss Wyckoff, whereas in the play, Rosemary is revealed subtly through the action. Rosemary drives home the theme that love requires humility.[23] It is, in Inge's play and in Inge's time, the woman who must be humble. This theme, viewed in the light of recent feminist critical theory,[24] is highly sexist and may be offensive to modern audiences. Nevertheless, the world in which Inge lived and about which he wrote, particularly in the small-town Midwest that provides the locales for his plays, was sexist. Most women had genuine status only as men's wives, and Inge's whole gallery of women, married and unmarried, reflects this predominant social outlook.

Rosemary's relationship to Howard also sustains another theme that pervades Inge's writing: What the world generally looks upon as love more often is the compromise that men and women are forced to make to keep from going through life alone. Rosemary compromises by marrying someone she does not love. Flo Owens's compromise was to marry the Hal type, a dashing, sexually appealing male who, after a short time, wanders off, leaving the woman with memories and children to provide for.

Rosemary adopts the rigid personality audiences see in her as the play begins. Her seeming rigidity is her defense. She abandons it quickly when she acknowledges that she must marry Howard or go through the rest of her life alone. Howard, forty-two years old, tells Rosemary he is set in his ways and that it is late for him to start changing. But Rosemary, who refuses to accept Howard's rationalizing, grabs his arm and tells him with assurance that she isn't young and that she is set in her ways, too, but that they need each other (*P,* 129–30). Rosemary's dialogue makes clear that she needs a home more than a man. She does not like to think about her age, but now must face it, must humiliate herself by discussing it, because she has no other weapons left in her arsenal.

In *Picnic,* much more than in *Sheba,* Inge is concerned with the pressures society forces upon people to keep up appearances. Because the conflicts of the major characters in the play are against society, Inge has to reveal to his audiences the kinds of power society exerts against its members to bring them into conformity to community norms. Helen Potts can ignore the wagging tongues of her neighbors when they wonder at her hiring someone like Hal to run around her yard half-naked doing his chores and at her allowing him to spend the night in her house. She fears, however, that these same neighbors might look upon her as rejected and lonely.

She sits down on Flo's porch and says that she could sit on her own porch but that she doesn't want the neighbors to see her alone (*P,* 88). She can bear all the frustrations of the dead-end existence she dutifully leads as long as she can project the impression that she belongs, that she is accepted.

Howard, too, is sensitive to what people think and to what local society demands, as many of his speeches indicate. When Rosemary asks him why he cannot dance like Hal, for example, he responds in *Summer Brave,* that if his customers saw him dancing that way, they would question his reliability (*SB,* 69). In *Picnic,* he has been inveigled into marrying Rosemary more for the sake of appearances than because he wants to go through life with her.

Inge uses Hal Carter's story of being picked up by some girls when he is hitchhiking and of being seduced by them to show that women have sexual desires, too, and to emphasize Hal's attractiveness to the opposite sex.

In *Summer Brave,* Inge makes Alan a college graduate rather than the college student he is in *Picnic,* thereby widening the cultural gap between him and Madge. Inge could have capitalized on this gap had he used it as a device for bringing Madge and Hal together in marriage. Even as he uses it, however, the device is effective, because in *Picnic,* Madge and Alan will not be able to marry until Alan has completed his studies, and it is possible, indeed likely, that Alan will outgrow Madge by that time. In *Summer Brave,* little stands in the way of their marriage, so the ending, in order to gain credibility, must separate them.

Alan, despite the cultural gap between him and Madge, is convinced that he loves her. He has never been successful with girls and, as Madge observes to her mother, he has an inferiority complex. He tells

Madge that the pretty girls put him off when he was at school because the competition for them was too great. He rationalized that he was too busy with his studies to care about girls (*SB*, 9). The implication seems to be that any union between Alan and Madge will involve a trade-off: Alan's money and position in exchange for Madge's good looks. Alan is clearly incapable of meeting competition, and Inge purposefully includes his speech early in the play to give the audience the wink that will let it know what the outcome of the Madge–Alan situation must be.

In *Summer Brave*, Inge cuts the part about Hal's having spent the night in Alan's car, thereby omitting the part about Hal's running away from the police. Instead, Hal spends the night in Helen Potts's house. The next morning Alan has a showdown with Hal and gives him money to leave town on the next train. This departure would be more satisfying than the one in *Picnic* had Inge retained those lines in *Picnic* in which Madge hears the train whistle and gives her speech about how train whistles excite her because she always thinks the incoming train might bring her Prince Charming into town. But Madge's Prince Charming will, according to her vision, not marry her and support her. Rather, he will find that she is just the person he is looking for to do some socially meaningful work in Washington, and he will spirit her away to do that work (*P*, 79–80). Inge scrapped these lines in *Summer Brave* and thereby sacrificed much of the impact of Hal's departure, which might ironically have come to represent Madge's dream in reverse. It is important to notice in both plays that, although Madge plans to marry Alan, she has not accepted the reality of this marriage, and she talks of escape, of being rescued, like the beautiful maiden in a fairy tale. In *Summer Brave*, she talks of going to New York or Chicago to be a model or an actress (*SB*, 12), and in both plays this talk of escape adds credibility to Madge's affair with Hal.

If *Sheba* established Inge's reputation as a serious American playwright, certainly *Picnic* assured the skeptics that *Sheba* had been more for Inge than just a fortuitous stroke. *Picnic* catapulted Inge into the big leagues by winning him three major drama awards, including the coveted Pulitzer Prize. People now put him in a class with Tennessee Williams and Arthur Miller.[25]

People in the Wind and Bus Stop

Bus Stop, an expanded version of Inge's one-act play, *People in the Wind*,[26] is a romantic comedy that unfolds when four bedraggled bus passengers—Bo, a ranch hand; Cherie, an entertainer; Virgil Blessing, Bo's guardian; and Dr. Lyman, a has-been professor—encounter a bus driver, Carl; a local sheriff, Will Masters; and two waitresses, the aging Grace and her young helper Elma Duckworth, in a corner restaurant at a way station somewhere between Kansas City and Wichita as they sit out a raging blizzard on a blustery March night. Inge got the idea for the play during the time he taught at Stephen's College, when he rode the bus between St. Louis and Kansas City most weekends. On one trip a vagrant young man was in avid pursuit of a girl whom he did not know. After every comfort stop he cuddled beside her and tried to talk her into getting off the bus with him when they reached Kansas City.[27]

In its dependence on a confined microcosm, *Bus Stop*—which might well have been subtitled "An Anatomy of Love"—is reminiscent of such earlier works as Robert Sherwood's *Petrified Forest,* John Steinbeck's *The Wayward Bus,* and Sebastian Brant's rambling fifteenth-century poem, *Das Narrenshyff (The Ship of Fools),* all of which depend upon a confined environment, a trap, to bring cohesion to their story.

Inge considered the play "only as a composite picture of varying kinds of love, ranging from the innocent to the depraved." He viewed the play as closer to fantasy than anything he had written.[28] In *Bus Stop,* he continues to pursue the theme of humility as a necessary concomitant of love, showing both the positive and negative sides of the theme.

In each of his two earlier Broadway productions, Inge's major protagonist was in danger of being overshadowed by a secondary character of sufficient proportions to be almost a protagonist. In *Sheba,* Lola is the major character, but Doc vies with her for the lead. The same is so in *Picnic,* where Hal Carter, the central figure, certainly has to contend seriously with Rosemary for the lead. Indeed, in *Picnic* the whole gallery of women forms almost a composite character that is important and significant.

In *Bus Stop,* Inge achieved the effect toward which his earlier plays moved irresistibly and progressively, that of producing a work in which several characters are of virtually equal importance, much as they are in Clifford Odets's *Awake and Sing!* and in other plays written specifically for the Group Theatre, whose philosophy of theater replaced the star system with ensemble casting.

The action of *Bus Stop* revolves around the pursuit of Cherie, a sexy, ungrammatical chanteuse—she pronounces it "chantoosie"—from near the Kansas City stockyards, by the crude but ingenuous Bo Decker, a young rancher from Montana, who insists on marrying the stubbornly unwilling sexpot because he has "been familiar" with her. One has the faintly amused feeling throughout *Bus Stop* that Inge is presenting a satire on conventional morality, that he has set up a situation in which he considers the obverse side of the conventional code.

Bo presses resolutely and with righteous indignation toward the forced marriage that will make him an honest man. The humor this situation engenders pervades the play and accounts partly for its popularity during a Broadway run of 478 performances and for the subsequent popularity of the Marilyn Monroe movie Twentieth Century-Fox based on the play.

As important as Bo and Cherie are to *Bus Stop,* all the other characters carry a full share of the burden in the development of Inge's exploration into the meaning of love. John Gassner labeled all the characters, aside from Bo and Cherie, secondary; viewing them, however, in the light of their roles as these roles contribute to the thematic development of the play, it would perhaps be more accurate to describe them, along with Bo and Cherie, as equivalent characters. The possible exception would be Will Masters, the sheriff, who is merely a utility character. Gassner says, ". . . some day, if left alone by producers, William Inge is going to write a play made up entirely of minor characters and come up with a major masterpiece."[29] Although Inge never did what Gassner suggested, it is interesting to speculate on what he might have written had he spent the 1930s working with the Group Theatre rather than being a student and then a teacher. A play like *Bus Stop* seems tailor-made for a company with the Group Theatre philosophy.

If *Bus Stop* is basically an anatomy of love, *People in the Wind,* from which it was derived, is an anatomy of loneliness. Inge's change in emphasis as he began to rework his original material is evident on even a cursory reading of the two plays. *People in the Wind*'s setting is identical to *Bus Stop*'s. In the earlier play, however, Inge hasn't time to develop the situation because *People* is a one-act play. In it the bus arrives during a storm but is not detained by the storm. What was a five-hour encounter in *Bus Stop* is a twenty- to thirty-minute rest stop in *People.* As a result, Inge had to deal in an attenuated way with the relationships that develop.

Bo and Cherie, who are identified merely as "Girl" and "Man" in *People,* receive the bulk of Inge's attention. Dr. Lyman, called merely "The Drunk," is pictured as a lonely man adrift. Somewhere in the

murky past, the girl he wanted to marry rejected him. Since then,
alcohol has been his comfort. Now, too shaky from drink to hold his
former teaching position, he spends most of his life on buses, riding
between towns.

The bus driver in *People* is a stock character, and Grace is more
hard-boiled than in *Bus Stop*. Elma Duckworth is the wide-eyed innocent
to whom things must be explained, giving Inge the opportunity to
reveal details necessary to the plot. Neither Will Masters nor Virgil
Blessing appears in *People*. The play, however, has two characters who
are not retained in *Bus Stop*, and this omission provides a major clue
to the shift in emphasis in the later play. These characters are identified
as "Old Lady 1" and "Old Lady 2."

The two women are presumably unmarried. They seem to be sisters,
although Inge does not specifically say. They are on their way to visit
Melinda, presumably their niece. One of them asks whether they can
afford to take a taxi from the bus station to Melinda's (*PW*, 138).
They are apprehensive about the reception Melinda is likely to give
them, speculating that perhaps they can help with the housekeeping
and not get in her way (*PW*, 146). These women, one of them drinking
bicarbonate of soda to settle her nervous stomach, represent what happens
in old age to those who have not formed close ties, a problem frequently
on Inge's mind.

The women loom before the unnamed Cherie and Bo characters as
one of two horrible examples of what can happen to people who go
through life alone. The drunk provides another face of loneliness in old
age. He prides himself on being a proud man, too proud to let the
woman who rejected him know how hurt he was (*PW*, 142). The
price Professor Lyman pays for his pride is clear at the end of the play,
where he acknowledges that he has nothing left in life but to ride the
bus (*PW*, 146).

Grace's cynicism and crassness in *People* are manifestations of her
loneliness. People pass through her restaurant by the dozen, but she
has formed no permanent ties with anyone and is portrayed as someone
in whom tenderness and warmth are mere memories replaced by the
defensive mechanisms she has constructed to protect herself from being
hurt. Her basic personality reminds one of Hal's and Rosemary's in
Picnic.

Elma Duckworth in *People* has no romantic complications to worry
about. She has just finished high school. In *Bus Stop*, Inge changes her
into a high school student, a girl who is just coming into an awareness

of what love is about, so that he can involve her romantically with
Dr. Lyman. Elma is bright, like Millie in *Picnic*. Her unpopularity
with boys is evident early in the play when Grace tells her that boys
might like her better if she didn't earn such good grades in school
because boys don't like girls who are smarter than they are (*B*, 8).
Elma, like Millie, wants to write a book about the people and situations
she sees (*PW*, 147).

The Bo–Cherie relationship in *People* is less convincing than in *Bus
Stop*. In the former Cherie complains to Bo that she does not know
him, that he is just someone who sat beside her on the bus and held
her hand (*PW*, 144). Cherie quails at the thought of going with Bo
to his ranch in Montana—but only because he has not mentioned
marriage. When he assures her they will marry (*PW*, 145), Cherie is
quick to follow him back to the bus. Furthermore, in *People*, Cherie
says she is heading for Hollywood and a screen test. Inge lets the
audience decide the veracity of her claim—does one ride the bus to
Hollywood if a screen test is assured?

In *Bus Stop*, however, Cherie has left her job at the Blue Dragon
and has no immediate plans. She hints she might go back to Kansas
City and work in a drugstore. Inge also makes it apparent in *Bus Stop*
that Cherie has about run out of money. She does not order two
doughnuts until she finds out how much they cost. When Elma tells
Cherie there is a good hotel down the street where she might spend
the night and get away from Bo, she tells Elma she's not a millionaire
(*B*, 14). In *People*, on the other hand, Grace tells her there is a small
hotel where she might stay but that she might have to wake someone
to check her in. Cherie says she doesn't want to be any trouble as a
pretext for her not taking a room (*PW*, 133).

Inge also builds background for the Bo–Cherie relationship in *Bus
Stop* by having Bo first meet Cherie in the Blue Dragon, where she
completely captivated him by her rendition of "That Old Black Magic."
Their simpatico leads them directly to the bedroom, where Bo loses
his virginity, causing him later to insist that Cherie marry him.

In *People*, Bo is crude and rough, and these qualities are attributed
to the fact that he, a rancher from Montana, is quite unused to the
cosmopolitan sophistication Cherie has been exposed to in Kansas City.
In *Bus Stop*, Bo is still crude and rough, but the audience comes to
know him well enough to be forgiving. Inge's creation of Virgil Blessing
also heightens Bo's characterization and makes him emerge as a lovable
person.

Virgil serves the dual purpose of providing the audience with background about Bo and of illustrating one of the forms of love Inge deals with in the play, the form the Greeks identify as *agathe,* a love based on charity rather than on eroticism. The name "Virgil Blessing" suggests the purity implicit in his devotion to the twenty-one-year-old Bo, whom he has looked after for the past eleven years. His name takes on added meaning at the end of the play when Virgil declines to return to Montana with Bo and Cherie but blesses their marriage.[30]

Dr. Lyman and Virgil represent polarities. Dr. Lyman's tragedy is that he has never had the generosity to love (*B*, 108); he is completely self-centered, realizes it, and is unable or unwilling to change. Inge reinforces Dr. Lyman's egocentricity by small touches such as one finds in the stage direction immediately prior to the beginning of his performance with Elma in the Balcony Scene from *Romeo and Juliet,* where Lyman shows he is a totally selfish performer (*B*, 98).

Dr. Lyman's nympholepsy reinforces the depth of his self-centeredness. On the other hand, Virgil is the soul of genuine, unostentatious sacrifice. His devotion to Bo is so sincere and ingenuous that he has passed up his opportunity to have a home and family. Yet, now that Bo has found the woman he wants to marry, Virgil steps out of his life with touching—if not quite believable—grace. As the play ends, Grace has to close the restaurant. It is five o'clock in the morning and the bus has left. Virgil has nowhere to go, and Grace tells him that she hates to see him left out in the cold. As the curtain is rung down, he says, "Well . . . that's what happens to some people" (*B*, 154).

In *Bus Stop,* Grace is warmer and sweeter than she was in *People.* Her attitude toward Elma, who in *Bus Stop* is younger than in the earlier play, is essentially maternal. Actually, in *Bus Stop,* Grace is to Elma as Virgil is to Bo. An obvious solution for both Grace and Virgil would have been for Grace to invite Virgil to share the warmth of her apartment and bed, as the bus driver Carl did earlier in the play. Each might have found the means of escaping the loneliness that now seems inevitable for both of them.

Inge, however, prefers to moderate the happy ending of his romantic comedy by adding a sardonic twist. The only person in the play who represents purity, with the possible exception of Elma, is left out in the cold, completely alone. His situation reinforces Inge's theme: life without love is lonely. Virgil has turned his back on conventional love and now, seemingly, he faces a life of loneliness (*B*, 70).

Dr. Lyman rationalizes his loneliness by equating it with freedom. The more he drinks, however, the further his inhibitions slip to reveal him as the most desperate character in the play. Inge surrounds him with an aura of mystery by making it clear that he is extremely eager to cross the state line (*B*, 19–20). Later, Carl and Will Masters have a whispered conversation about Lyman, and Dr. Lyman's situation is finally revealed clearly when he attempts to arrange a meeting in Topeka with Elma but urges her not to tell anyone.

In *People*, Dr. Lyman's nympholepsy is not presented explicitly, possibly because Elma is past the age of consent in the earlier play. Inge also reveals in *People* another facet of Dr. Lyman's personality that is not shown in *Bus Stop*. Dr. Lyman's retreat from painful realities is manifested in his excessive drinking, but how total this desire to retreat from reality is does not become apparent until the end of *People*, when Dr. Lyman equates the warm, encompassing bus with the womb, where he can sleep like a baby and to which he wants to return (*PW*, 146).

Some critics objected to the emphasis on sex in *Bus Stop*. Theophilus Lewis calls the play a "Decameron-type story of the Kansas plains,"[31] and Eric Bentley concurred in feeling the author might have toned down the play's sexual preoccupation.[32] Richard Watts, however, made the significant point that Inge is not writing about sex as a cheap, crass thing. He is using it, rather, to highlight the loneliness people experience, the searching they have to endure to find love and understanding.[33] The casual affair between Grace and Carl emphasizes the loneliness from which someone like Grace finds it impossible to escape. Near the end of the play, Grace tells Elma, who realizes that Grace and Carl have made love, that she is a restless woman who needs a man to keep her from getting grouchy (*B*, 151).

Inge uses the Grace-Carl sequence to heighten Grace's sense of lonely futility. Grace obviously has a reason for asking Elma to let her get Carl's meal. One of Grace's early speeches spells out her situation and her vulnerability to Carl quite succinctly as she tells how she hates to close up at night and go upstairs alone to her empty apartment (*B*, 6).

At the end of the play, the directions indicate that Grace performs the ritual of taking the garbage out and locking up for the night (*B*, 154). Virgil at this point has no place to go, but Carl has satisfied Grace's needs for that evening. The portent of what happens here is that her life will remain empty because, even though she is capable of kindness, she is not capable of sharing her identity with another person.

Bus Stop contains little action. The play is developed largely through talk, which Gerald Weales calls "the clumsiest exposition in the early Inge plays." He complains that "Elma Duckworth . . . wanders from character to character, gathering information as though she were a researcher for *Current Biography.*"[34] Weales's statement is justifiable, but the question remains of whether this technique is really a weakness. The device of using a central character in this way is common in drama. Gabby, in Robert Sherwood's *The Petrified Forest,* does much the same thing. In a play more dependent on thought than action, this method of presenting necessary information to the audience is efficient and hardly weakens a play dramatically. Inge handles Elma's gathering of pertinent information deftly, and one has no strong sense that this contrivance, as it is used to handle some of the play's necessary business, is forced or unconvincing. Inge protects against such an impression by the way he presents Elma. She is sincere and innocent, someone who enjoys talking to everyone, someone who is easy to talk to. The audience is aware of her character even before the bus arrives at the restaurant when Grace and Elma are together and engage in voluble conversation.

Inge prepares carefully for the delay that will force the bus's passengers and driver to remain in the restaurant for several hours. Early in the dialogue Grace says that the roads are passable to here (*B,* 4). Will Masters comes in and makes it clear that the bus will not get beyond the restaurant because the road west is blocked and might not be passable until morning (*B,* 9).

Inge also prepares the audience for the bus's lack of passengers by having Elma, as she looks out at the raging storm, tell Grace that she thinks the bus won't have many passengers because no one would go out on such a night (*B,* 5). Inge had to establish this point early in order to keep his cast small enough so that the dramatic structure of his play could succeed. With many more than four passengers on the bus, Inge would have had difficulty achieving focus. Had there been more passengers to serve, it would also have been impossible logistically for Grace to leave her station and go off with Carl.

In his portrayal of Bo, Inge produced a refreshing character, a completely innocent ranch hand as it turns out, despite Cherie's initial introduction of him before he enters suggesting that he is abducting her (*B,* 15). Her story is not wholly convincing because, in the next breath, Cherie reveals that Bo is asleep on the bus. In both *Bus Stop* and *People,* Inge prepares the audience carefully for Cherie's ultimate acceptance of Bo. In the one-act play, he makes it clear that Cherie was not entirely indifferent to Bo's initial advances. The two seemed to have enjoyed their kissing (*PW*, 143). In *Bus Stop*, Cherie does not deny her intimacy with Bo; she merely seems shocked that he should have taken a casual affair seriously.

Much of the play's humor is broad and stems from Bo's undisciplined, innocent approach to life. Bo is the prototypical provincial, the naive twenty-one-year-old just off the farm. He fully expects Cherie to jump at the opportunity to marry him when he tells her he loves her. The dialogue here is amusing but also touching because it has never occurred to Bo that he might love someone who did not reciprocate his love. Bo thinks that in a world full of crazy people who run around and kill each other, Cherie should embrace immediately the opportunity to marry him. When Will Masters tells Bo he is overlooking the fact that Cherie does not love him, Bo is dumbfounded and calls Will a "polecat bastard" (*B*, 53).

Bo is not a wholly sympathetic character until well into the second act when he confesses to Virgil that lately he has been barely able to cope with his loneliness (*B*, 69). This speech is akin to Doc's speech to Lola in *Sheba* just after he comes home from the drunk tank at City Hospital. Finally Bo recognizes that it is possible for a girl not to like him, and he is forced to begin a self-evaluation. In a series of speeches that would lend themselves well to musical comedy but that are also rollicking as straight drama, Virgil tries to tell Bo tactfully that he *might* succeed better with girls if he tried to be a bit more gallant, a suggestion that genuinely amazes Bo, who protests that he is as gallant as he knows how to be (*B*, 76). The good-natured banter in this scene is irresistible. The pace and timing are superb.

Even though Inge is not concerned essentially with the Bo–Cherie love conflict in *Bus Stop*, he makes it apparent early in the play that Cherie finds Bo attractive and suggests that she will not long resist his obvious adoration of her. When she takes part in the mock nightclub performance that Elma sets up, she sings the song that made Bo rapturous when he heard her sing it in Kansas City. Cherie, certainly, is contriving to use "That Old Black Magic" to cast her spell on Bo again. He reacts with all the vigor he displayed in the Blue Dragon when he first heard Cherie sing the song.

Cherie has a lackluster future ahead of her. Time is against her, and she knows it. She admits that eventually she will have to marry someone whether she loves him or not, and she talks cynically about how her attitude toward love has changed over the years (*B*, 81). Her speech

is the clincher because the audience already knows four things about
the situation that make the outcome predictable: (1) Cherie finds Bo
attractive; (2) Cherie is adrift; (3) Bo owns a ranch and has the makings
of a solid citizen; and (4) Bo has six thousand dollars in the bank.
Unless all signs fail in fair weather, Cherie will marry Bo. He is an
excellent catch for someone like her.

One might wonder why Inge made the outcome so clear in the
middle of the play. When he did so, he risked reducing the suspense
and weakening the dramatic structure of the production. Such would
be the case if Inge's chief concern had been with Bo's pursuit of Cherie.
Rather, Inge is concerned with using the Bo–Cherie conflict as an
example so that he can write more broadly about the question of love,
which is his concern for the remainder of the play. John Gassner was
correct in saying that the Bo–Cherie conflict "paid reduced dividends
as it went along."[35] He did not mention, however, that Inge used the
humor of the Bo–Cherie conflict—in the mid-1950s a quite unlikely
one—to sustain audience interest and reaction in the latter half of the
play, when his chief concern was philosophical and explored the broad
question of love.

The resolution of the central love conflict in the play comes only
after the man, Bo, has humbled himself. Will Masters, having had to
restrain him, has brought him back to the restaurant where he must
apologize to everyone. Bo finds it especially difficult to apologize to
Cherie, but he brings himself to do it after Will tells him, completely
in the Inge tradition, that people get the things they love by being a
little humble and that being humble is not the same as being wretched
(B, 119–20). Bo apologizes and then, as Robert Brustein puts it,
"indicates his tamed domesticity by solicitously putting his leather jacket
around her [Cherie's] shoulders,"[36] although one might ask whether
this act represented "tamed domesticity" or merely the behavior of a
basically good-hearted cowpoke whose acculturation is taking.

Bo, through his humility, has moved toward proving his point that
a person has the right to the things he loves (B, 119). Hal made a
similar point in Summer Brave when he called himself a poor bastard
(SB, 98). Bo and Hal are motivated by the same sort of impetuosity.
They all grasp hungrily for the love that can vitalize and give meaning
to their lives.

Bus Stop is a dramatically sound play. The time span of five hours
during which the entire action occurs imposed upon Inge the need to
provide a great deal of the background material through the dialogue.

He uses Elma Duckworth and Will Masters to draw necessary information from the principals in the play. The physical confinement of the restaurant also helps to bring dramatic unity to the action.

Despite its physical limitations, the restaurant is much less confined than the bus, and this element is emphasized by the illumination of the set, which calls for two ill-shaded light bulbs to hang on cords from the ceiling (B, 3). *Time* referred to Inge's bus as a symbol of "his whole lost, seeking, itinerant world."[37] But the bus also represents privacy for Bo and Cherie, and both security (the womb) and a means of escape (the journey) for Dr. Lyman.

The hope Inge offers audiences in *Bus Stop* is more upbeat than the hope Inge gave them in *Sheba*, which ends in a regrettable though credible compromise. Doc and Lola will suffer quietly for the rest of their days, held together by their weakness and by the absence of other reasonable options. Bo and Cherie, however, have come to fairly satisfactory terms with their situations. The physical attraction that they first found in each other may well develop into the sort of balanced love relationship that is a crucial ingredient in a successful marriage. Bo is loving and touchingly ingenuous. As the curtain falls, Cherie is beginning to appreciate him. She needs someone who will really love her because she has never known what it is to be wanted for anything except her sexuality. The virginal Bo can offer her what no other men have been able to—adoring, sincere devotion.

Inge suggests at the end of the play that Dr. Lyman, too, has changed and become more realistic as a result of the bus stop. He calls off his proposed liaison with Elma and comments that it feels good to do the right thing for once (B, 137). Although Dr. Lyman falls short of convincing anyone that he is really a reformed character, he at least leaves one with reason to believe that he is capable of being a man of some conscience. If his conscience has lain dormant for a while, at least it appears to have been reactivated by his five hours snowbound in the restaurant.

The play's most optimistic line comes at the point where Bo, shocked at the revelation of Cherie's past, reconsiders his desire to marry her. But, on reconsideration, he tells Virgil that he is pure enough for both of them (B, 142). Bo's love for Cherie is based on a realistic acceptance of what she is and of what her past has been. This realization leaves one with the feeling that their marriage will work.

In summing up *Bus Stop*, Henry Hewes wrote that Inge seems to have done "much more than interweave a trio of not very startling

sketches . . . they all deal with the conflict between security produced
by selfishness and true love." He continues, "The play's chief distinction
lies in the way Mr. Inge has served up banal characters with their most
sentimental fat trimmed off."[38] Inge's portrayal of emotions in *Bus Stop*
is stark and unsentimental, as his tightly controlled realism demands
even in a play that he regarded as being closer to fantasy than anything
he had previously written.[39]

Inge's clinical objectivity increased steadily from *Sheba* to the final
play of this highly successful period in his career as playwright, *The
Dark at the Top of the Stairs*. It was enhanced in each successive play
by his carefully unadorned use of language and by the classic starkness
of his settings. It is interesting that during the same period, Tennessee
Williams was moving toward more richly adorned language and increasingly complicated settings, and that Inge's plays were succeeding
whereas Williams's were not.

Inge was aware of what Brooks Atkinson terms "the illusiveness of
human experience."[40] Inge's characters often seek to overcome the
illusiveness to which Atkinson alludes by escaping from their loneliness
through sex. The sexual element in the Bo–Cherie relationship in *Bus
Stop* is initially not much different from that in the Grace–Carl relationship. One crucial element, however, put it on a totally different
plane: in Bo, love and passion merged into a single line, and it merged
in such a way that it was touching to Cherie, who, although jaded,
was actually a lonely girl in need of someone to love her as Bo could.
For the first time in her life Cherie is able to look forward realistically
to having a total, balanced relationship with a man who also needs
her.[41]

The Dark at the Top of the Stairs

Some critics have called *The Dark at the Top of the Stairs* a patchwork,
and this perception of the play reflects a critical misunderstanding of
what Inge was attempting. The play was Inge's most experimental full-
length production to date. His experiment was not wholly successful,
but the critics generally failed or simply refused to understand the
ramifications of what he had set out to accomplish.

John Gassner objected that "[t]he Jewish cadet's drama was dragged
in, and the play, sometimes veering towards comedy and sometimes
towards tragedy, was inconsistent in tone.[42] Actually, Inge strove specifically for what Gassner labels inconsistency in tone. The basic conflict,

the Cora–Rubin conflict, isolates each member of the Flood family. The conflict reaches its peak in the first act when Rubin quarrels with Cora because she has plotted behind his back to buy their daughter Reenie a new dress to wear to a dance. Cora goads Rubin into an anger that intensifies to the point that he strikes her and leaves, vowing never to return.

In the early stages of act 2 Inge allows the audience's attention to be divided. Cora is entertaining her sister, Lottie, and her brother-in-law, Morris, at dinner. She is frantic about her floundering marriage and tries to persuade Lottie and Morris to let her and the children come to Oklahoma City to live with them. But Cora has another immediate concern to deal with in this act: she has to get Reenie ready to go to the country club party that the newly rich Ralstons are giving for their daughter, Mary Jane.

The high point of act 2 occurs when Reenie's blind date, Sammy Goldbaum, arrives accompanied by another couple, Punky Givens and Flirt. Sammy is almost too good to be true—handsome, polite, considerate. Although the audience sees Sammy for only a brief interval in act 2, ensuing events in the play make him a central, though not major, character. When Sammy and the other young people exit, Cora and her guests return to their discussion of Cora's marital problems, admittedly an anticlimax—but that is exactly what Inge wanted.

The play's real climax comes in the middle of act 3 when Flirt rushes in with the news that Sammy Goldbaum has committed suicide. Inge follows this climax with a secondary climax by returning to the original conflict between Cora and Rubin. Just as the assembled characters receive word of Sammy's death, Rubin Flood comes home and tries to patch up his differences with Cora. Rubin enters the house without his accustomed boots, explaining to Cora that they are muddy and that he didn't want to dirty her clean house, the first sign that Rubin is becoming more considerate.

The divided emphasis of the play was disconcerting and distracting to some critics and to audiences, especially because the major climax does not appear in conjunction with its major conflict. Inge rationalized his technique by saying that he wanted to distract audience attention from the main story so that he could return them to it with a fresh viewpoint as the play ended. He declared that he was trying to show something about the universal secret fears that beset most people.[43]

Superficially, Sammy's suicide is the climax of the Sammy-versus-society conflict. One must examine this shocking act more closely, however, to understand how Inge chose to use it dramatically. Sammy's suicide brings Cora and Reenie to a new understanding of what life is about and to a deeper understanding of themselves. Certainly the suicide is the major precipitating factor in Cora and Rubin's being reunited.

Inge did an imperfect job of relating the two basic parts of *Dark*. The suicide itself is not wholly convincing. Inge tried, in words that take on a special significance in the light of his own suicide, to justify Sammy's rash act by explaining that he had never heard of a suicide that he had anticipated or that he had been prepared for.[44] But in this justification perhaps Inge errs by trying to explain and defend Sammy's suicide on realistic grounds. The suicide succeeds better metaphorically than realistically. In bringing the play to a resolution, it has served the artistic function that best illuminates its use.

Had Inge prepared the audience for the suicide by making Sammy a morose and maudlin figure, the act would have been more convincing realistically. Artistically, however, this approach would not have worked because the audience would not have been able to identify with a morose, maudlin Sammy in the way it did with the character Inge created. If the play is to work, the audience must have a closer identification with Sammy than it has with Punky Givens and Flirt, who accompany him to pick up Reenie.

Punky, like Sammy a military school cadet, contrasts sharply to Sammy. He remains in the background, slinking, mumbling unintelligibly whenever he speaks, a disappointing human being.[45] Inge juxtaposes Punky's withdrawn, sullen attitude to Sammy's warm, glowing personality so the audience will respond to each cadet with extremes of feeling.

The dark at the top of the stairs, from which the play's title comes, is staged realistically. Inge's directions specify in detail a flight of stairs at the far left of the stage, at the top of which is a hallway with no windows. Inge comments directly on the symbolic meaning of this darkness and of how threatening it is (3). Just as the missing dog became a controlling symbol of lost youth and lost innocence in *Sheba*, the dark at the top of the stairs in this play symbolizes the uncertainty and fear that all men feel. The dialogue makes the meaning of this darkened zone clear. Cora asks her son Sonny, who does not want to go upstairs alone, why he is frightened of the dark, and Sonny moans that up there you don't know what is before you—and it might be something terrible (79). As the second act ends, Cora and Sonny have started upstairs together into the fearful darkness.

After Rubin loses his job, he comes home and tells Cora what has happened. He says he is going to take another job, this time selling machinery. Then he reveals his own fears about the future, to which Cora responds that she never realized Rubin knew what fear was. Rubin then delivers a lengthy speech about the changes that have taken place in his lifetime. These include the increasing popularity of the automobile that has made Rubin's job of selling harness obsolete. He ends his speech by saying that he feels like an alien (100–101).

Rubin, too, is afraid of the dark, because it represents the uncertain future that stretches before him. But just as Cora assuages Sonny's fear of the dark by going up the stairs with him at the end of act 2, so does she assuage Rubin's fear of the dark (future) by going upstairs with him at the third-act curtain. This time, there is light at the top of the stairs, where Rubin stands waiting for his wife.

The parallelism between the endings of these two acts presumably marks the beginning of a healthier relationship between Cora and Rubin. Inge suggests that the oedipal problems between Cora and Sonny have been laid to rest and that Cora's marriage, which had been threatened by these problems, will now return to normal. However, this suggestion is difficult to accept when one considers the objective evidence throughout the play of the formidable oedipal situation between the two.

In *Dark,* Inge has built consciously toward an understanding and clear statement of the oedipal problem. He makes clear early that Rubin's frequent prolonged absences from home make Cora unhappy; she tells him she feels like a widow and that she is envious of women whose husbands do not travel (5). Cora's only real companionship is with her children. Because that companionship is all she has, she romanticizes it.

Rubin displays little real feeling for his children—partly because Cora has been so possessive of them that Rubin is unable to compete for their affection. He accuses Cora of possessiveness and, early in the play, shocks her with a story about an old mare on his father's ranch that refused to give birth to her colts and had to have them pulled from her (7). This speech dismays Cora because, on the surface it offends her delicate sensibilities, but deeper down because she knows it describes exactly the way she deals with her children. Rubin says outright that Cora fusses so much over Sonny that it would lead one to ask who is top man in the house (6). By the end of act 2 there is no question who is top man. After Rubin leaves, Cora tells Sonny that he is the man of the house now (79).

Sonny's jealousy of his father is another important factor in the development of the oedipal situation in *Dark*. Sonny wants his father to remain away once he has left his home and family. When Cora tries to reach Rubin by long-distance telephone, Sonny speculates enthusiastically that Rubin won't be there (78). Sonny is correct; Rubin is not there. Cora is disappointed, but then she hears a car outside, whereupon she dashes to the window. Again Sonny expresses his subconscious wish to have his father out of the way by saying it doesn't sound like Rubin's car, that it can't be Rubin (79). This is the same Sonny who, when Rubin strikes Cora and leaves, jumps up and down, shouting for joy (33).

Sammy reveals to the audience the oedipal problem in his life in the longest single speech in the play. It runs over half a page in print. He tells about his mother and her many marriages. He shows his utter isolation from anyone for whom he might be expected to care. But then he tells of two idyllic days he spent with his mother in San Francisco, of going out to dinner and a show with her, of dancing with her as though they were sweethearts (63). An almost identical theme pervades *Natural Affection,* in which Inge deals with the oedipal theme in a more direct way than he did in his earlier plays.

An especially tense encounter between Cora and Sonny resolves the oedipal problem in *Dark*. Cora confronts the problem by telling Sonny that he cannot come crawling into her bed any more. When he protests that he was frightened, she holds her ground and tells him that he is too old now to do that. She muses on the mixture she finds in Sonny, who is in some ways as shy as Reenie but in others very bold (90). This awkward encounter soon gives way to the play's most climactic scene, Flirt's revelation that Sammy has killed himself. This revelation is unique in American theater because it provides *tragic relief* from the intensity of the Sonny–Cora encounter.

Cora's frank conversation with Sonny takes place immediately after Sonny has returned from giving a recitation for which he has earned five dollars. This is the first time Sonny has been paid for anything, and he wants to use part of his money to go to a movie and to buy a big sundae afterward. But Cora takes the money from him and puts it into his piggy bank, despite his violent protests. Sonny goes into a tantrum—one of several he suffers in the play—in which he tells Cora that he hates her and threatens to kill himself (89).

Inge attempts to bring about the final resolution of the oedipal problem by having Sonny, in the last minutes of the play, take his piggy bank and, telling Reenie that it is his money and that he is not going to let his mother boss him, hurl the piggy bank against the fireplace in a fierce show of independence (107). Sonny thereby emancipates himself, emerges as a man. The solution, however, is not only too hackneyed, but it happens over too short a period to be any more convincing that is the oversimplified resolution of the oedipal problem in *A Loss of Roses,* in which one night of illicit love supposedly emancipates twenty-one-year-old Kenny.

With the possible exception of *Bus Stop* and *Where's Daddy?,* all of Inge's major plays have oedipal overtones. Both Lola in *Sheba* and Lottie in *Dark* are mother-wife figures, while in *Picnic* Madge is a mother-mistress type. *A Loss of Roses* is a full-fledged excursion to Thebes, and in *Natural Affection* Donnie's oedipal jealousy becomes the major wedge between Sue Barker and Bernie Slovenk as well as the precipitating factor that leads Donnie to murder.

Robert Brustein accuses Inge's women of wanting to tame their men, to make sons of them. None of Inge's men really rebels against this domestication except Rubin who, in *Dark,* walks out. But Rubin's rebellion is, presumably, short-lived. He leaves Cora because he does not want to be like his henpecked brother-in-law, Morris (102). When he returns to her, it is apparent that he will be tamed in much the same way Morris has been. A night in bed will neither alter the overall futility of the Floods' marriage nor resolve the problems that are responsible for Rubin's insecurities. Rubin is still out of work, and he shows no signs of being ready to settle into the sort of job that would enable him to have a close relationship with his wife or children.

Even at the end of the play, Rubin is unable to communicate with his son, and Inge does not suggest that this situation will change. From an objective standpoint, one must admit that the bulk of the damage in the Flood family has been done and that it is probably too late for its members realistically to expect any great improvement. Because her childhood has left her so much on the defensive, Reenie, even though she now recognizes her own selfishness, stands only a remote chance of ever finding anyone with whom she can really share her life happily. She tells Cora that she doesn't want to marry because she doesn't want to fight the way Cora and Rubin have (86).

Reenie is not unlike Laura Wingfield in Williams's *Glass Menagerie.* Inge wrote *Farther Off from Heaven,* from which *Dark* was derived, during a period when Williams was much a part of his life. In the early play, Reenie, like Laura, had a physical imperfection of which she was keenly aware: one of her front teeth was broken. This visible imperfection helped to explain a shyness so acute that the thought of going to Mary Jane Ralston's party with Sammy made Reenie sick at her stomach. But even without an obvious physical imperfection, Reenie's shyness is easily understandable because of her background.

Just as Laura sought to escape by means of her animals, Reenie attempts to escape by playing the piano—and Inge lets his audience know that she will not perform before anyone, that she plays just for herself, using her music solely as a means of personal escape. When Reenie becomes jealous at one point of the attention that Cora lavishes upon Sonny, she stalks off into the parlor to play a Chopin nocturne (34).

Reenie's shyness is indirectly responsible for Sammy's suicide. So upset was she by Mary Jane Ralston's party, where she felt dreadfully out of place, that she fled without telling Sammy she was leaving. Sammy looked everywhere for her (93). When Cora comprehends the situation, she minces no words with Reenie, telling her that she has to face life and that her shyness and sensitivity are nothing but selfishness (95).

Reenie finally understands the situation and her relationship to it in its totality. In misery at what she has come to realize, Reenie bemoans her insensitivity to Sammy, seeing how completely she failed him when he needed her (96). The change Sammy's suicide brings about in Reenie is symbolized by her telling Rubin that she has been practicing a new piano piece and asking him whether he wants her to play it for him (104). For the first time, Reenie uses her music not as a form of escape for herself but rather as a means of bringing pleasure to someone else.

The problem with Sammy's suicide is not so much its being shocking but rather whether it is worthwhile dramatically or realistically to have a promising youth kill himself so that a selfish, quite vapid teenager like Reenie can be enlightened by his death. In many of the situations that Brustein has identified as "men-taming," Inge seems rather to be suggesting that women use men, wittingly or unwittingly, for their own ends. Sammy was not tamed in the sense Doc or Hal or Bo or Rubin have been tamed. Rather he was sacrificed to the aggrandizement of the female, and Inge's use of Sammy forces one to reconsider his use in his other plays of other male characters who seemed initially merely to be tamed or domesticated.

Throughout her marriage, Cora has faced life almost as unrealistically as Reenie has. Rubin's frequent absences have increased her need to fantasize and romanticize. Her thought of living with Lottie and Morris and of finding a job in Oklahoma City is certainly unrealistic. Even assuming that she found a job—and with her lack of education and experience, she probably wouldn't—Cora could hardly hope to support herself and her children on what she might earn, particularly if she wanted to move as quickly as possible to a place of their own, as she assures Lottie she does.

Cora romanticizes shamefully when she implies to her sister and brother-in-law that Sammy has come all the way from California just to have a date with Reenie, a blind date at that (45), when the truth is that he has merely come from the neighboring town in which he attends military school. Cora offers little evidence in the play that she can face any sort of reality for more than a few minutes at a time.

One would expect that by this time Cora would know Rubin well enough to realize that he would never be content in the kind of job she envisions for him—running a corner grocery or being manager of a neighborhood chain store. It appears that this is the sort of occupation that Cora will try to push him toward, but Rubin has travel in his blood. He won't likely settle into the future that Cora wants for him— actually, the future she wants for herself. Every time Cora appears to be more realistic than romantic, she lapses back to her romanticizing and mouths romantic dreams that suggest she can give her children life wrapped up in a package that promises happiness. She will feel the same way tomorrow, even though all she can say to Rubin at this point is that she can promise the children no more than life itself (103).

The most confused character in *Dark* is Lottie. Indeed, in the light of what Inge reveals to audiences about each character in the play, Lottie's suicide would have been more plausible than Sammy's. Lottie has a basic, two-pronged problem: she is obviously sex-starved, and she has the simultaneous desire to master and to be mastered, the classic active-dependent personality. She is comparable to Rosemary in *Picnic*.

Lottie is a gross and vulgar woman. She stuffs herself with food, pulling the gizzard out of a bag of fried chicken so that she can gnaw on it (77). She most indecorously removes her corset in public and, rubbing her great fleshy stomach, proclaims how good it feels (76–77). Lottie claims to be disappointed by sex, saying that she has never enjoyed it (75). But for one who finds sex so disappointing, she is remarkably concerned that her husband has not touched her for three years (72). She obviously desires the attention more than the experience.

Lottie enjoys her fantasies of other men, and she never admits to herself the psychological overtones of these fantasies. She protests the suggestion that Rudolph Valentino is one of her favorite movie stars and claims that the only reason she saw him in *The Sheik* four times is that she wanted to keep her friend Marietta Flagmeyer company at the showings (49). But in the next breath, she admits her attraction to Valentino, simultaneously protesting that she would be afraid to have a man like that touch her (50), not that the danger was imminent.

Lottie is similarly ambiguous in her feelings toward Rubin, her brother-in-law. She tells of how Cora thought he was enticingly handsome the first time she saw him riding a black horse down the street (43). Then she admits to liking Rubin and tells Morris that Rubin has made a better husband than she expected him to but proclaiming that she is glad she is not married to him because she could not trust him the way she can Morris. But in telling Cora that if one has a handsome husband like Rubin, it doesn't matter if he is honorable, and then going on to tell a clearly phallic joke, she reveals her own inner conflict (71).

Vulgarity, Victorian prudery, bigotry, and self-righteousness—qualities often associated with severely sexually repressed people—are commingled in Lottie. So extreme is Lottie's bigotry that it becomes ludicrous. She suggests to Morris that he might like to marry the Catholic movie star Norma Talmadge and have the Pope run his life, join the Knights of Columbus and take an oath to kill all the Protestant women when the Catholics take over the world (48). Still a believer in the church militant, Lottie tells wild tales that have come to her thirdhand from Marietta Flagmeyer about how the Catholics keep arsenals in their church basements, stashed there against the day they arise to conquer the world.

Lottie is, of course, anti-Semitic as well as anti-Catholic. When she meets Sammy Greenbaum, however, she tells him that she and Morris don't think a thing about someone's being a Jew (57), but then she proceeds to advise him to join the Christian Science Church because she knows a former Jewish woman in Oklahoma City who was very unhappy until she became a Christian Scientist. She has been happy ever since (57).

Lottie is totally unfulfilled as a woman. She complains that she has no children, only a house full of cats. Cora reminds her that she never wanted children, and Lottie implies that she had said this only because she and Morris cannot have children (69). This problem helps to explain

Lottie's personality and allows audiences to feel a sympathy for her that they might not have otherwise.

Lottie serves a valuable dramatic function for Inge because it is she who delivers the line that expresses the thesis of all Inge's early plays. She tells Cora to get Rubin back even if she has to get down on her knees and beg him to come (70). The love-through-humility idea again suggests that if the marriage continues, it is because both parties have accepted the compromises necessary for its doing so.

Cora's marriage to Rubin, which has lasted for seventeen years, was originally based almost wholly on physical attraction, and it is such attraction that still holds it somewhat uncertainly together. Cora was pregnant by Rubin within two weeks of first meeting him. The two have little in common except the children and their physical attraction to each other. The breakdown in communication between them is apparent early in the play. Cora is so lacking in perception about her husband that she does not realize—or has never permitted herself to realize—that he is capable of fear. She, like her daughter, suffers from such basic insecurities that she cannot admit her husband's inmost weakness.

Cora's insecurities make it necessary for her to dictate to Rubin. When he comes home in good faith to beg her forgiveness for having struck her, he startles her, and her first words to him after a period of separation scold him for having frightened her (97). Within a few lines, during which Rubin reveals to Cora the bleakness of his present situation, Cora is again dictating, telling him that he cannot accept another traveling job and that he must talk to John Fraser about finding a job close to home.

Rubin, in his most assertive speech in the play, tells Cora that she cannot talk to a man like that. He tries to make her see that treating him as she does only makes him more rambunctious. He upbraids her for talking to him like the kind of man she wants him to be rather than like the man he is (99). In asserting his need for freedom, Rubin also shows Cora how their marriage might work.

In *Death of a Salesman*, Arthur Miller deals with the problem of how the Loman family became separated, of how it failed to communicate.[46] Inge is concerned with a similar problem in *Dark*. Rubin's separation from his children is partly an outgrowth of his feeling of alienation from his society. He wonders how he can offer his children anything when the world is so alien to him (101). Rubin's feelings, however, are also connected with his wife's feeling of separation from

him. Because Rubin is away from home so much, and because he is
a virtual stranger to his children when he is at home, Cora is overly
protective and possessive of the children, especially of Sonny. No real
spiritual communication exists between Cora and the children, however.
When Cora most needs them and when she most fears being alone,
Reenie retreats to the piano and Sonny to the movies or to his collection
of movie stars' pictures.

Until the end of the play, Sonny and Reenie are virtually cut off
from each other. Their bickering far exceeds the usual sibling rivalry
found in families, and this bickering is an extension of the behavior
the children have witnessed in their parents. The implication is that
the man-versus-woman contention they have been brought up with
could make it difficult, perhaps impossible, for them to make a normal
adjustment to life when they reach the marrying age.

The fact that Reenie and Sonny go off to the movies together at
the end of the play certainly is not enough to convince one that a
transformation has taken place and that from this day forward, sympathy
and understanding are going to replace the contentions between them.
They will be back at the same stands tomorrow, fighting and bickering
with each other, a fact that will likely drive Rubin back to the road
even if he and Cora have come to a better understanding of each other.

Cora's separation from her family is heightened by the coldness with
which Lottie receives her request that she share her home with Cora
and the children. In this scene, even though Lottie relents most reluctantly
at the end, one is reminded of the rejection Lola receives from her
parents in *Sheba*. In both plays, negative rather than positive forces
serve to bring about the domestic reconciliation. Whether these negative
forces can provide sufficient impetus to a force as positive as love is
highly doubtful. When people have lived in spiritual isolation for
seventeen years, as Cora and Rubin have, it is unrealistic to project the
simple solution to their difficulties that this play does.

Often Inge suggests that sex is the great leveler, as Williams does
with Stella and Stanley in *A Streetcar Named Desire*. Williams, however,
was realistic enough to portray Stella and Stanley during the early years
of their marriage. In the unlikely event that the Kowalskis were to
spend seventeen years together, they would probably have had to use
something other than sex to maintain their marriage or, as Williams
put it, to get "them colored lights goin'."

Sonny Flood is one of the memorable brats of modern American
theater. There is scarcely a moment in the play when one would not

be tempted to throttle the child. His mother has usually given in to his frequent tantrums, and her doing so has made Sonny well aware of what he has to do to get his way. He measures the intensity of each tantrum against the degree to which his mother is likely to resist it, and he always comes out the winner. Apparently Sonny comes honestly by his penchant to throw tantrums, if one of Lottie's lines, in which she comments on how Cora used to get her way with her parents, is to be believed (43).

Sonny's ability to recite does little to endear him to an audience already hard put to find any appealing qualities in the child. His recitations separate him from children his own age and suggest exhibitionism rather than real ability. The only recitation of Sonny's to which Inge exposes the audience is Hamlet's soliloquy (61), which is helpful both in reinforcing the oedipal theme and in introducing the subject of suicide, around which so much of the latter part of the play revolves.

Dark is sometimes out of focus both dramatically and structurally. Sammy's suicide is too dramatic, and it diverts attention too impellingly from the conflicts within the Flood family—which is essentially what the play is about. Inge's idea of diverting attention from the main plot so that it could be approached at the end with a renewed perspective is a good one, provided the new material does not eclipse the basic thematic material of the play. The suicide, however, is revealed so close to the end of *Dark,* and it has such an enormous impact, that the author has not left himself time to redevelop the main theme of the play in such a way that it can compete with the dramatic impact of the suicide.

As Inge unfolds his story, Sammy's suicide is more believable than many of the critics thought. The focus of the play is on the Floods. Only in act 2 is the audience introduced to characters outside the Flood family, save for brief appearances by Flirt in acts 1 and 3, when she brings information essential for audiences to have in order to understand what is happening. Sammy, however, dominates the first half of act 3, even though he is dead. His spirit becomes the most pervasive presence in the first half of that act, but Inge drops Sammy's presence all too hastily in the second half of act 3 so that he can return to his original plot and resolve it. It seems incredible that Rubin, upon his return, should be told nothing of Sammy's suicide and that the family should return to its routine so easily after such a crucial event had supposedly touched them so closely.

Many members of the theater audiences who saw the play had feelings similar to those expressed by John Gassner, who wrote that he "had little stomach for comedy after observing the suffering of the children and experiencing the penumbral mood of the scenes just past. It was impossible for me to put them out of my mind in watching the facile resolution."[47] Gassner also thought that Inge's "group play technique tends to dissolve this central drama in favor of peripheral themes, chiefly the mistakes that women make in trying to run men's lives. Everything Inge shows us here seems to be authentic, but his several truths weaken the one truth."[48] This criticism is applicable to *Picnic* and to *Bus Stop* as well, because in each of these plays, Inge allowed his themes to develop too permissively; too many minor themes compete with the major theme for attention. Perhaps this was Inge's way of being true to life, where things are not linear; but for many, the technique, when applied to playwriting, was distracting.

Some critics scolded Inge for relying so heavily upon clichés in *Dark*. This criticism seems ill-founded, however, because people like those about whom Inge was writing do ninety percent of their thinking and talking in clichés. To represent them otherwise would be to make their dialogue unrealistic and unconvincing. A more valid criticism, perhaps, is the claim that some of the dialogue is contrived. Lottie's garrulousness is used, as Lola's was in *Sheba,* to provide background for the action. The telling, however, is often too direct and is so sustained that the author's guiding hand is more apparent than it might ideally be.

Despite its imperfections, *Dark* remains one of Inge's most sensitive and perceptive plays in its depiction of common people trying to find their identities in a society that seems hostile and alien to them. Inge's forthrightness and delicacy endeared him to audiences. His work is, as Richard Hayes has put it, "full of the pleasures of recognition."[49]

The Impositions of Success

From 1950 until 1958 William Inge rode the crest of a wave that seemed to have no downward trough, a truly remarkable feat. Each of his new plays represented a high-water mark for him. His career, unlike those of many artists, advanced steadily, unabated, for nearly a decade. But a decade of success, especially at the beginning of one's career, turns an artist into a public monument, and once the tradition of success is established, a hungry public presses artists to further production, ever challenging them to improve upon themselves.

Established authors who fall short can either rationalize and vow to do better in the future, thereby leaving the way clear for their next creations or, as Inge did after the failure of *A Loss of Roses,* strike out against a fickle public and defend their work. In either case, they feel pressured and bear a degree of humiliation for having pleased less than they were able to in the past.

Robert Brustein called Inge a "fiddle with one string."[50] If his statement has a degree of truth, one must remember also, that Inge, to carry the musical analogy further, spent much of his productive life writing variations on a theme, which is quite different from being a fiddle with one string. Each variation has had its own appealing freshness.

If one cannot always agree with Inge's suggestion that modern man's redemption is through sex and through showing humility in love relationships, at least one must recognize that a significant number of unlikely relationships between men and women are initiated and perpetuated on a sexual basis. When the initial sex interest fades, relationships often are held together through the sorts of compromises that Inge imposes upon most of his characters.

Chapter Three
A Loss of Affection

"I like things always to be sweet as possible."

—Lila in *A Loss of Roses*

With the closing of *The Dark at the Top of the Stairs,* Inge's star was still in the ascendant. Random House had published *Four Plays by William Inge* in 1958, and William Heinemann was negotiating to bring out the British edition that appeared in 1960. Inge had a new play, *A Loss of Roses,* almost ready for Broadway, and it was widely assumed that this play would be successful, as his last four had been.

Inge felt particularly good about the new play because *A Loss of Roses* was a completely new original script. Twentieth Century-Fox paid $200,000 for the film rights before the play opened at the Eugene O'Neill Theatre in New York on 28 November 1959. As it turned out, *A Loss of Roses* was badly received, and the critics attacked it savagely. The play closed after twenty-five performances, and Inge, who was its largest backer, lost a great deal of money as a result of the production's failure.

More important than the financial losses that Inge incurred, however, was the effect the rejection of the play had upon him. Inge was never able to detach himself from his work to the extent that he could consider harsh criticism of something he had written as anything other than harsh criticism of him as a person. He realized at a conscious level that he had this attitude. Even before *A Loss of Roses* opened on Broadway, Inge said that some vital part of authors go into anything they write and that if their work is rejected, they, too, feel rejected, even scorned.[1]

Marilyn Mitchell writes of Inge, "He, who had himself been both a teacher and a critic, could never casually accept criticism, and this was part of the tragedy of his career . . . his obsession was to be accepted, and the fact that his last works were not, probably contributed to his death."[2] Janet Juhnke offers another dimension of Inge's dilemma after *Dark,* writing of how *New Republic*'s critic, Robert Brustein, attacked *Dark* brutally, along with all of Inge's earlier writing, in a much circulated, extremely venomous article in *Harper's,* "The Men-Taming Women of William Inge."[3] William Gibson, in his eulogy shortly after Inge's death, recalls how totally destroyed Inge appeared to be after he had read the article in which Brustein charged that Inge's plays "wallow in commonplaceness."[4] Brustein reviewed all of Inge's subsequent plays scathingly, writing like one consciously out to destroy a sensitive artist. Brustein's reviews disturbed and distressed Inge enormously, as well they might have coming from a man who then was a renowned professor at Columbia University and who was later to become dean of Yale University's School of Drama and still later director of Harvard's prestigious Loeb Theater.

In a letter written a year after Inge's suicide, his sister, Helene Connell, says that as his days ebbed, Inge thought he had lost his ability to write and that writing was the only thing that mattered to him. In his own eyes, he had nothing to live for.[5] Inge had not lost his ability to write, as he had feared, but the criticism he read of his work, particularly Brustein's, caused him to think of himself as ineffective.

Damning first-night reviews of *A Loss of Roses* caused Inge to flee almost immediately from New York, first to Nashville and then to Florida for a vacation. He left New York, not like a petulant child who was not getting his way, but rather like a badly wounded, sensitive artist who needed to leave the scene of his failure so that he could reassess his future, his writing, and his role as a major American playwright.

Inge now decided to switch to a new medium. He began work on a film script and finished it quickly. Warner Brothers distributed *Splendor in the Grass* in 1961, and the script won Inge an Oscar. Inge had felt geographically and artistically constricted in New York, and, for the time, working on film scripts in California gave him the kind of change he needed. At first he reveled in his new medium, making full use of the flexibility and fluidity it permitted. For a while, he felt like the sculptor who has switched from marble to clay or like the painter who has switched from water colors to acrylics.

His career as a script writer, however, was short-lived. The theater was too much in Inge's blood for him to turn his back on it, so before 1962 was over, he had returned to New York to help put his new play, *Natural Affection,* into production. The play opened at the Booth Theatre and lasted for thirty-six performances. It seemed incredible to Inge, to the critics, and to audiences that the celebrated playwright of the 1950s had now had two failures in a row.

Most critics of *Natural Affection* had at least some good things to say about the play. In their virtually unanimous reservations about it, they objected that, although the first half of the production had a satisfactory pace in which Inge effectively built suspense, the sensationalism toward the end of the play negated the well-controlled first half and weakened the dramatic structure so severely that it made the play artistically unacceptable.

One can only speculate on the sort of reception *A Loss of Roses* and *Natural Affection* might have received had they been Inge's first two Broadway productions rather than his fifth and sixth. It is likely that *A Loss of Roses,* as a first play, would not have gone into production until Inge had rewritten the script to make Lila the major character, a change that would significantly have strengthened the production, perhaps to the point that Inge would have been heralded as a promising new playwright.

Natural Affection, despite some of its profoundly moving vignettes, merely suggests the author's real gifts. As an early work in the Inge canon, it would have given evidence of his promise and potential. Coming, as it did, however, after four major successes and one failure, *Natural Affection* caused critics and audiences alike to view the play as the death knell of a considerable talent.

Inge again returned to California to make a film script of his short play, *Bus Riley's Back in Town,* an adaptation of *Glory in the Flower,* an earlier short play. Universal Film's 1965 production of *Bus Riley* deviated so much from Inge's script and the production so displeased him that he had his name removed from the credits. Shortly after the film's release Inge wrote, "As for *Bus Riley,* the picture is a loss. I took my name off it. I haven't even seen the version they are showing."[6]

Inge was to have only one more play produced on Broadway. *Where's Daddy?* opened at the Billy Rose Theatre on 2 March 1966 for a disappointing run of twenty-one performances. Throughout his lifetime, Inge's plays continued to be produced off-Broadway and outside New York City. However, *Where's Daddy?* marked the end of his career as playwright, despite the few one-act plays he wrote between 1966 and his death in 1973.

A Loss of Roses

A Loss of Roses is about the depression of the human spirit. If Inge was adversely criticized for pursuing a redemption-through-sex theme in his earlier plays, he must now be called to task for writing a play in which sex fails to suggest redemption in any satisfying or convincing way. Although sex crystallizes the basic oedipal problems of the two principal characters, Helen Baird and her son Kenny, if Inge intends to leave the audience with the feeling that Kenny's one night of love with Lila, his former baby-sitter, will solve his problems, he is guilty of extreme oversimplification.

In this play, as in his earlier ones, Inge gives his audiences false hope, asks them to accept a basically untenable solution to the problems he puts before them. The play consistently misleads audiences into believing that Kenny's umbilical cord is made of tougher stuff than the play's pat conclusion suggests.

Inge's preoccupation with the Oedipus complex, which pervades *The Dark at the Top of the Stairs* in subtler ways than it does in *Loss*, becomes the central psychological concern of the play. The central male character in *Loss* is Kenny, a twenty-one-year-old who is in many ways Sonny Flood come of age. The sibling rivalry that sharpened the lines of conflict in *Dark* is missing from *Loss*. By doing away with the sibling rivalry and by making Kenny an only child, Inge gains more ground than he loses. *Loss* avoids the annoying bickering between brother and sister that pervades *Dark*. Also, in *Loss*, Inge is in greater control of the mounting tensions between mother and son than he was in *Dark*, where these tensions were sometimes diluted by Reenie's presence.

But Inge also created problems for himself by unfolding his story in this way. The Kenny–Helen conflict is so intense and so free from the distractions that reduced the intensity of a similar conflict in *Dark* that the roles of Kenny and Helen overshadow Lila's role, even though Inge intended that role to be equivalent to the roles of the other two principals. The film version of *Loss*, *The Stripper*, was more artistically satisfying than the Broadway version simply because Lila emerged as a stronger and more pervasive character in the film.

If *Loss* is largely the story of an only child, it is certainly the story of an only child with two mothers. The only way available to Inge if he was to make the psychological conflicts in the play convincing was to create in Lila a woman at once alluring and attractive, yet quite a bit older than Kenny. She is thirty-two years old in *Loss*, eleven years Kenny's senior. Inge makes his portrayal of Lila as convincing as he can by casting her as an actress who demonstrates early in the play that she can attract men. In introducing Lila, Inge calls her a voluptuous blonde, uncommonly beautiful. He comments on her sincerity and generosity of spirit,[7] suggesting qualities that one might seek in a mother surrogate.

Inge emphasizes that Lila is a mother surrogate by reiterating throughout the play that Lila used to be Kenny's baby-sitter, that she regularly looked after him when he was a small child. One of Lila's early speeches to Kenny establishes her as the mother figure that Inge wants the audience to envision. She reminds Kenny that he used to call her his Aunt Lila, that she used to give him his bottle and change his diapers and bounce him on her knee. She goes so far as to say that she was a mother substitute for him (24).

Later, when Kenny is reminiscing, he tells Lila that he remembers more about her, about how she used to indulge him, whereas his mother was quite strict (41). The situation has changed little. Lila is permissive throughout the play. She waits on Kenny, she keeps his confidences, she feels empathy with him when Helen rejects his anniversary gift to her, and she eventually capitulates to his advances after his mother has hurt him. By now she has deluded herself into believing that Kenny will marry her.

Even though Inge deals more openly with the Oedipus problem in *Loss* than he did in *Dark,* the characters in *Loss* seem less consciously aware of the problem than Cora did in the earlier play. Even though Helen shrinks from Kenny when he tries to kiss her and tells him that he is too old to "make love" to her the way he did as a small child (13), she is not forceful with him as Cora is with Sonny after he creeps into her bed. Generally in *Loss,* direct acknowledgment of the Oedipus situation is skirted rather than stated outright, often being suggested by double entendres such as that found in the dialogue between Lila and Helen after Kenny has given his mother a wristwatch for her wedding anniversary, a gift that she has rejected:

> HELEN: I can't let him do things like his father did, Lila.
>
> LILA: But every boy wants to be like his father.
>
> HELEN: There are some ways he can't be allowed.
>
> LILA: But a *present* . . . that he wanted to *give* you. (81–82)

This portion of dialogue serves two important functions. First, it indicates Helen's recognition, conscious or subconscious, of the existence of the oedipal problem. Second, by telling Helen that she could never be hard to Kenny, Lila prepares the audience for her final capitulation.

The entire play builds up to the climactic seduction scene. In building toward this climax, Inge uses many secondary details to illustrate the problems between Helen and Kenny and to make their existence plausible. Lila has been on stage for only a few minutes, for example, when she remarks to Helen how much Kenny looks like his father (23). This observation comes to mind instantly when, a bit further along in the dialogue, Lila confesses to Helen that she had a crush on Kenny, Senior (32). Obviously, this is Inge's forewarning that Lila will transfer her crush to Kenny. Lila's earlier statement also helps to explain some of Helen's own fears about allowing her son to be too loving with her.

Helen and Kenny bicker quite a bit in *Loss,* but their bickering has more point to it than the bickering between Sonny and Reenie in *Dark.* It indicates the tensions that have built up between Helen and her son, while it also serves to illustrate the strong love that exists between them, for most of their quarrels end in some display of affection, some affirmation of their love for each other. Helen struggles throughout the play against her own possessiveness. She wants to be independent, and she has convinced herself that she wants to free Kenny from her so that he can lead his own life. Her nagging, however, is a manifestation of her possessiveness, which she is incapable of overcoming quickly.

Helen has some reason to harbor deep-seated resentments for Kenny and this resentment occasionally boils over, often articulated indirectly when the two are bickering. Kenny has twice deprived Helen of the fulfillment that she might find in love and marriage. It was in saving Kenny from drowning that Big Kenny himself drowned, leaving Helen a widow with a child. After her husband had been dead for some years, Helen had the opportunity to marry another man, but she did not do so because Kenny objected (52).

Kenny is actually more possessive of his mother than she is of him. His objection to her remarrying illustrates this in part, but his continued possessiveness is seen also in his desire to have her quit work and stay at home, to be largely dependent upon him. The very things that Kenny wants of his mother come to be supplied by Lila, who washes Kenny's socks and cooks elaborate meals for him. Lila's taking over such duties emphasizes her role as surrogate mother, and Inge works steadily to enhance this image of her. At one point, for example, he has Lila tell Kenny that he doesn't have to apologize to her because she is not his mother. Kenny responds that he has forgotten she is not his mother (41), foreshadowing what is to come. Later Helen says to

Lila that she is just the other mother Kenny has wanted to pamper him (76), reiterating the building up of the play's oedipal theme.

The wristwatch symbol is vital to the psychological impact of the play. It would have been well for Inge to do more with this symbol rather than using the contrived and seemingly tacked-on symbol of the roses at the end of the play. While she is reminiscing with Lila, Helen tells her that she still has the watch her husband gave her for their fifth wedding anniversary (32). The audience later learns that this watch, now some seventeen or eighteen years old, has stopped and that Helen intends to have it repaired.

The high point of the play's action comes when Kenny spends over fifty dollars to buy his mother a new watch for her anniversary, which she still celebrates as one of the few things she has left to celebrate (73). Lila has prepared a festive dinner for the occasion and has mixed some drinks. When Kenny comes home, he shows Lila the package he has for his mother, as well as the receipt for the watch.

As act 2 opens, before Helen arrives home for her anniversary dinner, one has the feeling that Lila and Kenny are playing house like two children. Lila, a small-time actress with little recent experience in domesticity, enjoys this unaccustomed opportunity to keep house. The festivity of the occasion has raised her spirits. She and Kenny dance to the music on the radio. Lila pretends that they are young lovers, but she does so in apparent innocence. Kenny finally gives way, however, to the desire that has been growing in him during the time Lila has been there. He begins to kiss her passionately on the mouth.

When Helen comes home, she is tense and obviously suspicious of what has been going on. She sees that Kenny and Lila have been drinking together and is aware they have been dancing. These indications of intimacy make her uneasy, but she controls herself. Kenny's giving her the watch he has bought her, however, is more than she can stand. The presentation of the gift serves as a triggering device to her emotions. Helen will not accept the gift. This rejection and disappointment cause Kenny to say that he is going to leave home.

Lila's dinner is left untouched as Kenny stamps out. The watch symbol is fully realized just before Lila leaves the Baird household. Kenny, who has now made love to Lila, gives her the watch, signaling that he has now abandoned his attempt to replace his father in his mother's life and that, through Lila, he has found the solution to his complicated oedipal problem. However, Inge arrives at this solution so suddenly that the audience is not prepared for it. It seems, therefore, to lack credibility.

Lila is the most compelling character in *Loss,* largely because her psychological development is authentic and believable, although it is at times presented in such oversimplified terms as to lack the full dramatic intensity it might have. Lila's beginnings and early background are obscure. The audience learns that her mother lived until Lila's unfortunate marriage and subsequent suicide attempt. Lila's single statement about her mother, indicating she is relieved that her mother is dead and not trying to run her life for her (47–48), provides an interesting parallel to Kenny's feelings about his mother. Lila's statement, of course, is pure rationalization; what she is really saying is that no one really cares about her. Although she is a free agent, she doesn't want to be.

Inge deals with this point later in the play when Lila's lover, Ricky, is about to arrive. Helen suggests that the two of them might want to spend the night together. Helen appears to be a broad-minded, understanding friend who can make such a suggestion to Lila without any embarrassment. The truth of the matter, however, is that Helen is eager to get Lila out of the house because she has to work all night and she does not trust Lila to be alone overnight with Kenny, who might return.

Helen tells Lila that even though she is religious, she is not a prude. She says that she realized immediately that Ricky was Lila's lover and was not about to sit in judgment of anyone (83). Lila tells Helen that she is wonderful, but one wonders if she says this with any conviction. As Lila is portrayed, she needs and wants someone who will tell her the rules of the game and force her to obey them. She is painfully aware that no one really cares enough about her to set up any prohibitions against her promiscuous behavior.

Lila acknowledges her emotional immaturity and confides to Helen that she often feels like a child who might do silly things when she is afraid and wants someone to be close to her (85). She concludes this speech by admitting that anyone will do when she is afraid of being alone and that sometimes she hates herself.

Lila's basic insecurity is intensified when Helen takes no moral stand against her affair with Ricky, as a mother might do. Yet Inge cannot permit Helen to take such a stand because if she did, she would be playing mother, and Inge's presentation of Lila as surrogate mother would be vitiated. The more nearly Inge can present Helen and Lila as equals, the more control he has over the development of the oedipal theme in the play.

One may question why Lila enters *Loss* as she does with a band of characters who are not necessary to the development of the plot. These seemingly superfluous characters show Lila in the milieu she is about to leave. They represent a world considerably more sophisticated than she will find in small-town Kansas with Helen and Kenny. Also, having Lila arrive with this band enlivens a dinner scene that involves only Helen and Kenny, a scene that Gerald Weales has described as "one of the dullest passages in the Inge canon."[8] The need for immediate contrast is apparent. The question is whether this band is rollicking enough to provide the contrast that Inge needs here. Lila's friends consist of Madame Olga, a lusty but quite hackneyed grande dame; Ronny, a stereotypical homosexual, who has been playing juvenile roles for twenty years and whose libido on occasion has to be put down by Mme Olga's stern authority; and Ricky, a wooden character who plays heavies and who, besides being Lila's lover, is her unofficial manager.

Weales knew what the production needed at this point: "Some big, boozy theatrical caricatures that might wake up the play."[9] Although Inge had a good idea in introducing Lila's friends, he did not capitalize sufficiently on it. His dialogue in this scene is pedestrian, whereas, had it been outrageous, it could have produced the desired effect. The basic situation would have lent itself to exuberant wit, but instead Inge's dialogue trudges along. Actually these supernumeraries temporarily block the play's development rather than enhance it. The only function they serve is to emphasize that they are leaving Lila behind in a wasteland.

Inge also fails to capitalize on Lila's loneliness when she is left at the Bairds. Indeed, she plunges rather volubly into conversation with Helen, and they relive together parts of their common past, some of which gives the audience necessary information. One does not have the feeling that Lila is any lonelier here than she would be anywhere else. She seems to have learned to live with loneliness and personal isolation. Lila's personal isolation often surfaces during the play but never so clearly as when Helen suggests that Lila try to make friends outside the Baird household and urges her to call on Mrs. Mulvaney, a neighbor she thinks Lila would like. Lila resists the suggestion, explaining that she is shy with people and that she has little in common with married, church-going mothers like Mrs. Mulvaney (74).

The play offers no evidence that Lila has ever really tried to establish any common ground between herself and other people. Her permanent sense of loneliness brings about her affair with Kenny and makes her almost plead with him to marry her afterward. Lila seems never to have been in control of her own destiny, as the ending of *Loss* makes clear. Ricky, her lover, is himself desperate and can do little to make Lila feel more secure. He finds sexual gratification in her and nothing more. Marriage is not a part of his larger plan and, even though he is a flat character in the play, his unscrupulous and disreputable nature comes through resoundingly.

Ricky finds Lila a job in movies, but after he has built up her hopes, he lets her know that he has arranged for her to work in pornographic movies and to do a degrading nightclub act as well. When Lila refuses, he threatens to blackmail her and also abuses her physically to get her to accede to his scheme. Kenny enters, quite melodramatically, and Ricky runs off. But after her affair with Kenny and after a halfhearted suicide attempt, Lila realizes that her only reasonable solution is to do what Ricky has proposed. He comes, at her bidding, to take her to Kansas City to an uncertain, presumably unsavory future.

After the Broadway production of *Loss,* Inge realized that he should have concentrated the ending of the play on Lila's departure, thereby focusing more attention on her than on Kenny and Helen. With Shirley Booth in the role of Helen, however, he could not very well make the change. During rehearsals, Booth demanded rewrites that would emphasize her role even more. By the time Booth had left the company after the Washington tryouts, explaining that she felt Lila's role overshadowed her own, Inge was in a corner. Betty Field was brought in hastily to replace Booth, and the play either had to go into production in New York before it was ready or to incur unmanageable expenses while it was revised extensively for Broadway.

As the play was produced, the anticlimactic scene between Helen and Kenny runs its course after Ricky has whisked Lila away. The last scene reinforces what has already been strongly implied: that Kenny has freed himself from his oedipal problem and that he is now free to leave home and live his own life. However, Inge divided audience attention in the last scene by introducing into its last minutes Mrs. Mulvaney and her small daughter, an intrusion that seems clumsy and unwarranted.

Sandra Mulvaney represents the young innocent. The sight of the little girl off to her first day of school launches Lila on the most unfortunate bit of dialogue in *Loss.* Lila recounts her story of taking roses to her teacher on the first day of school and of how the teacher ended up slapping and scolding her. Inge seems here to be equating roses and innocence, but if he is trying to suggest at this juncture that the theme of the play is the loss of innocence, he is misleading his audience. Innocence has been lost long before the opening curtain. The play's theme has to do with the great depression of the human spirit, a situation that there is little means of ameliorating. One just learns to live on, making what compromises are necessary in order to continue an existence that never seems worthwhile.

Inge's attempt to free Kenny from his oedipal tie to his mother is a central issue in the play. He gives audiences every indication that Kenny does not want to leave home. He prefers to be an automobile mechanic and to live with his mother than to take a much better position he has been offered in Wichita. The surface conflict between Helen and Kenny grows out of the strength of their feeling for each other. Kenny, exhibiting a Madonna complex, has little respect for any woman except his mother. He shuns opportunities to get to know socially acceptable girls, preferring to date the loose kinds he can pick up at the skating rink.

When Jelly Beamis accuses Kenny of getting what he wants from girls then discovering that he hasn't any money to treat them, Kenny tells him that he won't waste his money on the kind of girls they pick up (16). Jelly upbraids Kenny for never taking anyone to the movies but his mother. Kenny answers that he doesn't put girls they pick up in a class with his mother. His feelings are clear later in the play when he tells Lila of his dream of doing something for his mother because he feels he owes it to her for having kept her from remarrying. He says he feels sorry that she has to go through life without a husband (62). Then he spews out his feelings in a dialogue that sounds like a *Reader's Digest* essay on motherhood (63).

Inge drives home the point of Kenny's liberation by having him tell Lila of the troubled dream he had during their night of love. In it his mother dies (98). This dream can easily be interpreted to mean that Kenny has killed his mother, in which case his decision to leave home becomes inconsistent. In waking and finding the dream is untrue, the guilt that it suggests should be diminished. The relief that Kenny would feel on discovering that he had just had a dream and that his mother is all right would seem more likely to keep Kenny in his trap than to free him from it.

Kenny's dream seems less valid in its psychological implications than Lola's dreams in *Sheba* were. Her dreams explain her conflicts and indicate clearly their resolution. Kenny's dream serves no such purpose and only churns the already muddied waters.

Most of Inge's characters are caught up in zestless existences. The settings of his plays—stark, simple, monotonous—promote the effect, as do the frequently zestless responses of his characters. Kenny often is characterized by his almost defeated answers that things are "OK." In *Sheba,* Lola responds to occurrences with an almost identical lack of enthusiasm, frequently saying, "That's nice." This sort of lackluster reply indicates the spiritual bankruptcy that Inge sees in many of his characters. They withdraw emotionally into a virtually anaesthetized state that appears to be their only protection from pain.

In *Loss,* Inge plays, sometimes quite remotely, with various sex themes. The oedipal theme, of course, is the most fully developed of these. He hints at a homosexual theme when he introduces Ronny into the play. He has Lila tell of her peculiar relationship with her husband, Ed Comiskey, whose father, posing as Ed's brother, tried repeatedly to seduce her. The Lila–Ricky affair is fundamentally sadistic. Inge also implies a sexual basis for Kenny's kleptomania. Kenny steals relatively valueless objects—gloves, an empty change purse—but always from women.

Helen Baird's reaction to hearing about the sexually complicated lives of the people in the tent show in which Lila acted during her marriage to Ed Comiskey is a clue to some of her deepest sexual fears. She expresses shock, says that she has never heard of such people and would have reported Mr. Comiskey to the police as a degenerate (45). Helen, of course, *has* heard of such people, but she prefers to turn her back on the reality that they exist, just as she prefers not to acknowledge consciously the real problem in her own life. Helen is a strong woman, but a major concomitant of her strength, arrived at arduously, is the rigid personality she exhibits. Underlying all of her strength is a pervasive insecurity not unlike Inge's.

Loss suffers from a lack of inner motivation. Much of its action is dissipated in talk, and the talk is not always convincing. Some false notes serve to reduce the play's credibility.[10] The amateurishness of some of the psychological presentation is at times misleading. *Loss* is the first Inge play to use its characters primarily for presenting plot. Previously the author permitted characterization to predominate in his plays. Plot and theme were natural outgrowths of his strong characterization. In this play, however, Inge seems to have begun with plot rather than with people. The characters become servants to the plot, and the theme develops willy-nilly.

Perhaps the play's greatest structural flaw is that is presents two basic stories, each worthy of its own play: the Helen–Kenny story and the Lila story.[11] He never brings these two stories together into the unified whole that his earlier plays were. Where he has tried to weld them together, the seam shows.

Splendor in the Grass

Splendor in the Grass is a warm and perceptive psychological study of two adolescents who are deeply and passionately in love. The two must control and restrain their love until the boy is ready to go into business as his father wants him to. The story is set in eastern Kansas and most of it takes place before the stock market crash of 1929. A few anticlimactic scenes occur after the crash, and the final scene takes place presumably in 1933 or 1934. The period covered, then, begins with prosperous times, when oil was discovered in Oklahoma, bringing wealth to it and to its neighboring states, including Kansas, and ends with the dust bowls that afflicted the same area in the early 1930s. The economic events of the period are roughly parallel to the emotional situations of the two principals in the film, Bud Stamper and Wilma Dean Loomis, generally referred to as "Deanie."

Ace Stamper, Bud's father, is a self-made man whose oil company is experiencing unparalleled success. As the action begins, a new gusher has just come in, and Stamper stock has risen fourteen points in a day. Ace, however, is an unhappy man. His only daughter is a nymphomaniac who causes him pain, not because of his concern over her situation, which is desperate, but because he fears what people will say and think about her. Bud's wife is not a realized character in the film. In her few scenes, she reminds one of the protagonist in Evan Connell's *Mrs. Bridge*. Bud is his father's only real hope for the future. Ace idealizes him as representing all that is worthwhile in life. Bud is strong, is the star player on the football squad, and seems capable of continuing the course his father is now charting in the oil business. Ace dreams that Bud will go to Yale, then will return to become an executive of Stamper Oil.

All Bud wants in life, however, is to study agriculture at the state "cow college" and run his father's ranch. Bud wants to marry Deanie and dreams of doing so before he goes to school so that she can accompany him. Bud's plans obviously conflict with Ace's dreams for him.

Deanie is a sweet, genuine girl. Bud is her whole life. She can conceive of no future that does not include him. She is willing, nevertheless, to wait for him to finish Yale if that is what she must do. Deanie's father, Del Loomis, a small-town grocer, is a sympathetic and sensitive man. Although Deanie's mother is a garrulous, domineering woman, she, too, is basically sympathetic. Deanie appears to be an only child, although Inge never specifies that she is.

As the film opens, Del Loomis is experiencing his first limited taste of prosperity because he has bought some Stamper Oil stock that is appreciating with a whirlwind momentum. Although the economic gap between Bud and Deanie is substantial, the cultural gap is hardly noticeable because they both come from simple, small-town families, one of which is newly rich, the other modestly comfortable.

Inge might have created a Montague–Capulet type of conflict in his script, in which case the plot would have been contrived and predictable. But Inge's Ace Stamper is no Montague. He is too practical to fight openly the love situation between his son and Deanie. He does not forbid Bud's marriage to Deanie, but rather tells him that she is a nice, good-looking girl.[12] Later, however, he tells Bud that all he cares about is having him finish Yale, after which he can certainly marry Deanie with Ace's blessing and with a honeymoon trip to Europe thrown in as a wedding gift (29). Beyond all else, Ace is a realist. He knows that to forbid marriage only precipitates it, whereas to delay it will likely destroy any chance of its ever taking place.

Ace also leads to the destruction of the pure and happy relationship that Bud and Deanie have by telling his seventeen-year-old son that for now he needs another kind of girl to help him get off some steam, not the sort of girl one marries, but the sort one uses (29). Ace, the crass, practical businessman, cannot understand Bud's idealism—or, if he understands it, he prefers to redirect it. Even though Bud is not shown as having any overwhelming respect for his father, he is obviously influenced by Ace's advice, which inevitably affects his relationship with Deanie.

Ace's dealings with his son are far from admirable. He plays on the boy's sympathy and elicits from him the sort of behavior he wants by making Bud feel that he controls his father's happiness. Ace, ever aware of being a self-made man, drives this point home by telling Bud that he has to run for both of them because when he was about Bud's age, he fell off an oil rig and injured himself so that he had to stop running (8).

When Ace speaks about his daughter, he reminds Bud of what a disappointment she has been and tells him that now all his hopes depend on Bud (9–10). When Bud broaches the topic of marrying Deanie and going to an agricultural college, Ace does not rant and rave. Rather he tells him tragically and melodramatically that he cannot face another disappointment (29). Ace's statement, of course, is complete tripe. He would adjust to Bud's marriage in a week, and as a grandfather, he would be obnoxiously boastful. He is not, however, above using any tactic he can to direct and control Bud's life.

Ace is the film's most important secondary character, and Inge's portrayal of him is masterful because he resists the opportunity to write Ace's part merely to fit the stereotype to which he corresponds. Inge never loses an opportunity to develop Ace as a round character. A totally materialistic person, Ace cannot understand that Bud and Deanie are in love. He has probably never been capable of the kind of love Bud and Deanie feel. A number of his statements show that for Ace, love and sex are synonymous.

Ace knows full well that sex is for sale to anyone who has the price. He also thinks that everything and everybody has a price. When Bud is ill with pneumonia and it appears likely that he will die, Ace tells Doc Smiley that he will receive a five thousand dollar bonus if he saves Bud's life (53). Such statements reveal Ace's standards. He can be bought and has been. He can also buy when he has to.

Ace has no legitimate grounds for wishing that Bud will not marry Deanie—except that at this time, it was not usual for married men to attend college full-time. Certainly there was no financial barrier to Bud's marriage. Although he never actually says so, Ace probably objects to the marriage because he thinks that Bud will soon be able to make a much better marriage than this one.

One might have expected Ace to reconsider Bud's marriage to Deanie after Bud has nearly died of pneumonia. Ace, however, is so convinced that material things can cure any wounds of the heart that when Bud leaves the hospital, he gives him a new car rather than allowing him a new way of life. Inge uses this new car to precipitate Bud's affair with Juanita, and this affair leads to the breakdown of Bud's romance with Deanie.

Ace is ever the realist. Through Bud he lives vicariously the youth of which he himself was deprived. Ace attempts to foist on Bud all he thinks he would have wanted as a youth; but in so doing, he is trying to shape Bud to the socially approved mold. Yale is a fundamental part of this mold, and Ace is desperate when it becomes clear to him that Bud is not going to succeed at Yale.

Ace's suicide is amply prepared for and is convincing, indicating that Inge took to heart some of the criticism of Sammy's suicide in *Dark*. Throughout the film, Ace Stamper has two basic motivations—material success and sanguine expectations for Bud. He loses both of these motivating factors simultaneously. Having interfered irrevocably with Bud's life, he does the only thing he has left to do: he plunges from a hotel window to dash himself to death on the pavement below. His action is both expected and impetuous. On the night of his suicide Ace takes Bud to Tex Guinan's nightclub in New York. Guinan in the floorshow makes light of the very thing that Ace is soon to do, saying that on her way to get her taxi she had to dodge the bodies of people leaping from windows (101). Ace, who has drunk too much, tells Bud that he is not going to be around much longer. He hastens to add, however, that he has no immediate plan to die (102). Within a short time, however, Ace is dictating a suicide note to a prostitute he has brought back to his hotel from Tex Guinan's club. Minutes later, he is dead.

Ace's death marks the end of Bud's career at Yale, a career that was about to end anyway. But now the Stamper family is bankrupt. Bud manages to save his father's ranch from the creditors, and he returns to it to live the life he had wanted to live in the first place. Now, however, there is a major difference. He cannot have the life he had envisioned with Deanie because she is in a mental institution. He marries an Italian girl, Angelina, of whom Ace would have approved much less than he approved of Deanie.

Bud bears broad resemblances to Biff in *Death of a Salesman*. After Ace dies by his own hand, Bud, the appealing young athlete, gives way to a Bud whom Deanie describes as being like any man anywhere, just trying to survive (120). The idealized Bud is gone.

Left to his own devices, Bud was a remarkably uncomplicated character. He was not very strong, but he was devoted and dutiful both as Deanie's fiancé and as Ace's son. When his duty to his father came into conflict with his duty to Deanie, Bud could not resolve the dilemma, and Deanie lost by default more than by any action on Bud's part. Inge might have done more to show the extent of Bud's conflicts. He reveals them to some extent early in the script when he has Bud go down the hall of the high school slamming locker doors and creating a great deal of noise. The direction that accompanies this action indicates that Bud does not understand his own feelings or the violence he has felt within himself lately (16).

Again, when Bud is playing football, he tackles an opponent with a crushing blow. The directions say that a furious official lunges at Bud and penalizes his side for unnecessary roughness (19). The climax of the film would have been better realized had Inge included more instances of this sort of behavior in Bud.

Inge's understanding and recording of adolescent behavior is nothing short of amazing. The small touches that were almost entirely lacking in *Loss* are present with vigor in *Grass*. The great irony of the story is that Deanie and Bud are living in strict accordance to conventional codes of morality, even though to do so is incredibly difficult for them. The adults they look toward for understanding are either ineffectual in helping them solve their problems or are openly suspicious of their relationship. When Bud pleads with Doc Smiley to give him some sort of guidance in solving his problem, all Doc Smiley can do is evade his questions and offer him vitamins and a sun-lamp treatment (55), thereby escaping the dilemma.

Deanie faces a problem with her mother, who asks her if she and Bud have been physically involved. Deanie assures her mother that they haven't, but asks her mother if it is terrible to have sexual feelings toward a boy. Her mother replies that nice girls do not have such feelings and goes on to propound the hypocritical philosophy that Inge has always been concerned with exposing by telling Deanie that Del never touched her until they were married and that she gave in to it just because she had to. Sex is not something nice women enjoy (4). Although she is well-meaning, Mrs. Loomis makes Deanie feel as though her feelings for Bud set her apart from nice people, make her a pariah.

The scene fades and shortly shifts to the Stamper home, which stands in sharp contrast to the Loomis's small house. Ace interrogates Bud in much the way Wilma Loomis has interrogated Deanie (8). Both Deanie and Bud are humiliated even though they suffer the pain of unfulfilled passion and have fought to maintain the standards of morality that their families have so fumblingly tried to impose upon them.

Inge is particularly effective in *Grass* when he depicts high school scenes. He obviously knows and understands what kinds of people one finds in a high school, both adolescent and adult—the teacher whose own sexual frustration makes her jealous of any signs that her students

have found fulfillment; the girl students who hold in awesome esteem
a girl who, like Deanie, has found the elation of complete identification
with another human; the slithering, insecure, oversexed Juanita; the boy,
Toots, who doesn't know what love is but who has a keen sexual
awareness and has found that Juanita is an easy means of satisfaction.
Other touches such as the whispering in the back of the classroom
have remarkable authenticity. Inge catches the exact cadences of these
clandestine conversations and has made them contrapuntal to the classroom recitation that is going on simultaneously.

The river becomes a point of reference in the scenario and is used
with good dramatic effect. The action opens with a passionate necking
scene between Bud and Deanie, who are in Bud's car beside the river.
This part of the local lovers' lane is specifically their territory, a fact
made clear when Bud brings Juanita to the same place but, realizing
where he is, suggests that they move to another place. At the river,
Bud also makes his declaration to Toots that Deanie is now fair game—
Toots declares that, because Bud is no longer dating Deanie, this is
his chance. When he asks whether Bud objects, Bud answers hopelessly
that he cannot stop Toots (62). The answer is clearly one of defeat,
Bud's attitude for the rest of the film.

The river is especially significant in the development of the story
because the film's climactic scene, Deanie's attempted suicide, takes
place there. Toots has taken her to the spring prom where she sees
Bud for the first time in several weeks. Determined to end the suffering
and uncertainty she has been enduring by offering herself to Bud, she
goes to the parking lot with him. Inside the car, Deanie cries, begging
Bud to take her sexually, proclaiming that she wants him (75–76).
Bud, who cannot bear to put Deanie in a class with Juanita or with
his nymphomaniac sister, rejects her advances. His rejection is more
than Deanie can bear, so she bolts from the car, runs away, and plunges
into the river. This act confirms her father's opinion that she should
be placed under a doctor's care in a psychiatric hospital. Deanie is sent
to Wichita for treatment, and Bud leaves for Yale, each having been
forced to yield to the forces that separate them. In the hospital, Deanie
meets the man whom she finally marries just to keep from being alone.
In New Haven, Bud meets Angelina, the understanding waitress whom
he marries.

When Bud stops seeing Deanie, she is in a more unhappy circumstance
than Bud, who can at least look forward with some hope to the future:
he will go to college and, as far as he knows, he will one day be in

command of his father's growing enterprises. Inge says nothing of Deanie's future. He leaves this point vague because Deanie's future without Bud *is* vague, a fact that makes her a sympathetic character to the audience and that also makes her suicide convincing.

Ironically, Ace tells Bud after Deanie's suicide attempt that he is fortunate not to be tied up for a lifetime with someone who is obviously unstable (84). The suicide and the attempted suicide emphasize the two basic values at work throughout the film: Deanie, an idealist, attempts to end her life because of love; Ace, a materialist, ends his life because he cannot face his inevitable financial failure. To Ace, his reason for suicide is the only justifiable one. He never understands the force of love, and this is his tragedy. Even his feeling for his son is one of possession rather than love.

If numerous critics condemend *Loss* because it talked itself to death, they certainly could not make a similar judgment about *Grass*. Writing about *Dark*, Harold Clurman said that Inge "writes sparsely, almost laconically, but his choice of words and of situations is so shrewd that he makes them go a long way in creating a stage life far more potent than the written page may indicate."[13] One might make exactly the same observations about *Grass* in which Inge consisently draws the rein tight on his dialogue and presents the content of the play with sensitivity and subtlety.

In *Loss*, Inge supplies background material somewhat clumsily by having the principals provide each other with information they would already be expected to know. When he needs to supply similar information in *Grass*, however, he does it by having the characters talk almost to themselves, to muse about the past.

Inge is never guilty of overwriting in this work, as he sometimes was in *Loss*. In his scenario, he has returned to the crisp dialogue of *Picnic* and of *Bus Stop*. He treats his situations deftly and prefers to suggest rather than to elaborate. One might note, for instance, the economy of the two hospital scenes: the first, when Bud is ill with pneumonia; the second when Deanie has attempted suicide. The first is used primarily to show that Ace thinks he can buy anything including the life of his gravely ill boy. Inge achieves the effect he needs in seven clipped speeches between Doc Smiley and Ace, after which he shifts the scene to the church where Deanie is praying for Bud's recovery. This shift, which emphasizes the difference between Ace and Deanie, sketches deftly the impression that Inge wants the audience to form of each. The author tells the audience nothing; rather he has the characters

show through their actions what each is. The long speeches in *Loss* are replaced by clipped dialogue and compelling interaction among the characters.

The second hospital scene is longer than the first, but it serves a manifold purpose. It shows Mr. and Mrs. Loomis's differing attitudes toward Bud, and it marks the play's real climax. The climax begins really with Deanie's decision to go to the dance and ends with the announcement that Deanie must enter a psychiatric hospital. In the crucial hospital scene, Bud finally decides to defy his father and marry Deanie. He declares that he is of legal age and will do what he wants to (83). But Doc Smiley tells Bud that it will be a number of years before Deanie is ready to marry anyone. At this point, dramatically at least, the movie ends. Circumstance has now forced the decision toward which the film has been working, and everything that follows it is both anticlimactic and dramatically unnecessary.

One might ask whether Inge made too great a compromise in continuing the play beyond the second hospital scene. It is unlikely that he would have written further had he been writing for Broadway audiences. However, the larger and less sophisticated film audience is concerned with outcomes, and Inge had to bow to this popular preference. He succeeds in building toward a second climax in the final meeting between Bud and Deanie. In this scene, Inge writes a typical Hollywood ending, quite different from any of his Broadway play endings.

Sex solves nothing in *Grass* as it does in some of Inge's earlier plays. Instead everything is solved by the passage of time, by Deanie's recognition that Bud is like other men. Had the film ended with the second hospital scene, the ending would have been essentially a romantic one. Ending as it does, it moves from the romantic to a mildly pessimistic determinism suggestive in some ways of the naturalists. This ending is by no means a Thomas Hardy or Frank Norris ending because it is not so decisive as an early naturalist would have made it. To the extent to which Inge is naturalistic, he is naturalistic in a minor key. Death is not the ending here. Instead, as in Inge's earlier plays, the principals have made the compromise that will enable them to go on living.

But in his earlier works, Inge made the compromise a bit more palatable. In *Bus Stop* and *Dark,* certainly, Inge suggests by the ending that sex can overcome all difficulties. One does not have this impression at the end of *Grass.* Bud and Angelina are eking out an existence and raising a family, but Bud will never know real love again.

Even were Bud to win Deanie again, he could not know the love for her that he once did. He has passed beyond that period in his life. He is a different person; Deanie is a different person. Deanie will marry the young man whom she meets at the psychiatric hospital, but she has experienced the one all-consuming love in her life. She can not relive it.

In films, Inge was able to shift easily and gracefully from scene to scene. Such flexibility is impossible on Broadway even on a stage with revolving sections. In the film, Inge was able to touch on points briefly for illustration and then leave them to move on to something else. The pace and forward thrust of his film story distinguish it from any of his other work. Despite the length of its anticlimax, *Grass* marks a new vigor in Inge's work. He has wedded poignancy and understanding with effective dialogue and well-conceived characterization. His total result is promising and, in itself, highly effective.

Natural Affection

Natural Affection opened at the Booth Theatre on 31 January 1963 and closed after thirty-six performances. The play, seriously flawed toward the end, might easily have been salvaged. Had it been cut halfway through the second act, much of the sensationalism that begins when the Brinkmans come to Sue and Bernie's apartment on Christmas Eve would have been eliminated, making possible a resolution without Donnie's senseless murder of a stranger at the end of the play.

Inge contends that he was writing of things as they really happen, just like the lurid events one reads about in the newspaper every day. He tells of an actual case like this one,[14] and that case must have been in his mind for some time because elements of it are found in his depiction of Hal's background in *Picnic*.

Certainly any casebook in psychiatry records instances of the sort of senseless and brutal murder Donnie committed. Drama, however, remains an art form and, as such, audiences expect it, even when it seeks to be realistic, to be different from newspaper reporting in that it selects and presents its material with full attention to artistic effects and to anticipated audience response. In its last minutes, *Affection* replaced real drama and genuine dramatic effect with sensationalism and vulgarity. The Greeks long ago realized that some of the gory details of tragedy are better reported than shown.

The artistic question *Affection* poses is whether a playwright should show everything that might actually happen or should leave some things to the imagination. In writing of Odets's *Till the Day I Die,* Edith Isaacs objects to the author's showing a Gestapo officer smashing the hand of Ernst Tausig, a violinist. She wrote that she hoped Odets would "come to know . . . that an audience can feel longer and more deeply the pain in a violinist's mutilated hand if they see the effect of the hammer blow upon it instead of seeing the blow itself."[15] Isaacs's statement is broadly applicable to *Affection.* Certainly an author has the right to present events as they actually happen. The question is one of how a playwright chooses to present such truths. Inge had a strong play until he overemphasized its sensational elements, thereby making *Affection* too direct and too literal for audience acceptance.

The play's title, of course, alludes to the affection a mother feels for her child. In this case, the mother, Sue Barker, is a beautiful, thirty-six-year-old woman. The child is her son, Donnie, illegitimate and now seventeen years old, who, having been brought up in an orphanage, has never known the kind of affection most young children experience. His mother has been devoted to him, but for many years she has not been able to care for him because she had to work. The audience is told how she used to visit Donnie in the orphanage and of how he used to cuddle up to her lovingly.

When Sue finally became successful as a buyer for a large department store, she was able to take Donnie to live with her. Soon Donnie got into trouble and was sent to the work farm, a type of reform school. The play opens on the morning Donnie is to return from the farm to spend the Christmas holiday with Sue. During Donnie's absence, Sue has moved into the luxurious apartment of Bernie Slovenk, a Cadillac salesman some years younger than she.

As the play opens, Sue has risen early from the bed she shares with Bernie and stands staring out the window. Bernie asks her what she is doing, and she answers, setting the mood for much that is to follow, that she is looking out at the world and that it looks ugly (4). Inge consciously used this line to prepare the audience for the ugliness that is to follow (vii). He restates the line near the end of the play when Sue again stands looking out the window and comments on the ugliness of the morning (106). *Affection* has about it the overall bleakness these lines suggest.

The beginning of the play is brief and focuses largely on Sue's reaction to Donnie's homecoming. She anticipates conflict between Donnie

and Bernie. Bernie is uneasy about Donnie's arrival. No one is in the
apartment when Donnie arrives with Gil, another boy from the work
farm. Gil appears briefly so that he and Donnie can engage in conversation
necessary to reveal to the audience some of Donnie's problems at the
work farm. He has had problems with a homosexual guard, and he
expresses to Gil the hope that he will be able to stay home with his
mother rather than return to the farm.

Bernie is the stumbling block to the fulfillment of Donnie's dream.
Sue needs Bernie sexually. It is clear from the start that he has no
thought of marrying her. At this point in his life Donnie needs Sue if
he is to lead any sort of satisfactory existence, but his presence puts a
strain on the relationship Sue and Bernie have established. The resolution
of the conflict comes when Sue reaches her decision after she has made
a genuine effort to be a dutiful mother. She cries out to Donnie that
she isn't going to sacrifice the rest of her life for a worthless kid she
never wanted, and tells Donnie to stop hanging on her (144). As soon
as she has uttered these words, Sue tries to take them back, but it is
too late. The damage has been done. Sue exits, and a drunken woman
wanders in from the party next door looking for Bernie. Not finding
him, she turns her attention—and affections—to Donnie. He reaches
for a carving knife and stabs her to death on stage.

Affection has stronger oedipal overtones than anything Inge had written
previously, although he explored the theme in both *Dark* and *Loss.*
Inge establishes the oedipal theme early in the play when Donnie first
comes into the apartment. He goes into his mother's bedroom and
fondles her clothing. Later, when Bernie leaves, Donnie, like Kenny in
Loss, tells his mother what a happy life they can have together. He
tells her that he loves her now as he always has and that he can offer
her as much company as Bernie can. He tries to kiss her, but she
rebuffs him (112–13). The oedipal situation is heightened by the fact
that Donnie is a virtual stranger to Sue, who at thirty-six is attractive
and has a lover younger than she.

Affection's strong subplot explores the relationship between Claire and
Vince Brinkman, the couple who live in the apartment across from Sue
and Bernie. Bernie has had an on-and-off affair with Claire. When he
doesn't want her, he sends friends of his to have sex with her. Claire
is a vital and sensuous woman. Vince, some years older than she, is
rich, impotent, and has homosexual feelings for Bernie.

Vince, although not quite an alcoholic, drinks regularly and lives
frenetically to block from his mind the hopelessness of his marriage to

Claire and of his life in general. During his one drunk scene, reminiscent of Doc's drunk scene in *Sheba,* his dialogue is as sexually frank as any dialogue to reach the New York stage up until that time. The subplot presents a sharp contrast between the illicit love that Sue and Bernie share and the more socially condoned love that the married couple, Claire and Vince, share. The final scene makes clear that Sue and Bernie really love each other but that Claire loathes Vince, who loves her very much.

Inge portrays Sue as a woman who has risen to a high position in her company because she has a strong sense of responsibility and is naturally bright. Her feeling of deep responsibility to Bernie is heightened by his losing his job through a mischance on the very day that Donnie comes home. Nothing could have set the scene for conflict better than Bernie's being fired.

Sue also feels a strong responsibility toward Donnie. She conceived him out of wedlock and the father disappeared. Rather than have an abortion, she carried Donnie because he was hers. She would not terminate the pregnancy. She realized her responsibility, and that realization made her strong (16). She calls Donnie's infancy the best time in her life despite her poverty (18). Sue's feelings toward Donnie frighten and threaten her. Just as her responsibility to Bernie is heightened by his being unemployed, her responsibility to Donnie is increased by the knowledge of what he is suffering at the work farm. His back is scarred from a severe beating he received from the sadistic, homosexual guard who gets his pleasure from beating the boys in his charge (42).

Bernie is likable, but he lacks Sue's native intelligence and ability. He is in love with her, and his love is sincere. He is rankled at making less money than she, and he realizes that Donnie poses a threat to their relationship, making him resent the boy before he has met him.

Donnie is concerned about Bernie and wonders whether Bernie will like him. He discusses this problem with Sue, and she tries to reassure him. Inge, however, places every possible obstacle between Donnie and Bernie to assure their not getting along. Donnie arrives home in old clothes and has to wear some of Bernie's clothes when he goes downtown to buy some clothing for himself. When he wears Bernie's favorite cashmere jacket and his vicuña shirt, Bernie is greatly annoyed, the more so because just before he meets Donnie for the first time, he wrecked a brand-new Cadillac, which resulted in his being fired.

Bernie arrives home feeling desperate and hopeless. His irritation mounts as he discovers successively that Donnie has worn his clothes, has left the bathtub filthy, and plays rock-and-roll albums on the phonograph at full volume. It is obvious, as well, that Donnie and Bernie are competing for the affections of the same woman. To make it worse, their rivalry must remain sub rosa. In this rivalry, Donnie has the upper hand because he can ask with seeming innocence questions about whether Bernie ever pays for anything (71). But Donnie has even a stronger hold over Bernie; he has caught him kissing Claire Brinkman passionately in the kitchen (86). What's more important is that Donnie, as Sue's natural son, has prior claim to her. Try as they might, Donnie and Bernie can never be friends. The intensity of the competition between them is too great to permit friendship. Inge must use their rivalry as a means of forcing Sue to make a choice between them, and whatever choice she makes, she will lose something dear to her.

Donnie has had a hard life. He is at the work farm because he and some other boys stole a car and because he beat up a woman in Lincoln Park (12). Within the first few minutes of the play, Inge shows some of the manifestations of Donnie's aggressions, which he presents so specifically that the audience has a forewarning of what might happen as the play unfolds.

Inge shows Donnie's reaching out for love as well as his sexual precociousness. Sue reveals to Bernie that when Donnie was only fourteen he was living with an old whore who was buying him clothes (13). All of this is buried deep in Donnie's past. He is presented on stage as a handsome, appealing, sometimes touching youth. He craves Sue's love with unusual desperation because the alternative to his winning it is to return to the work farm.

Donnie has to be ruthless in his competition with Bernie. He fights with any weapon at his disposal. He tells tales on Bernie, and in his last desperate bid for his mother's affection, he tells her that Bernie is only after her money but that he would double-cross her without a second thought (111). Sue realizes that possibly there is some truth in what Donnie says, and this fear makes her uneasy. Such taunting precipitates the outburst that leads to the play's final drastic action. Even though Sue is a strong woman, she is not sufficiently sure of herself nor does she have the inner security to allow her to have Bernie's love for her questioned. Donnie's attempts to behave properly are used throughout the play to indicate how important he thinks it is for him to remain at home.

In his first appearance with Gil, Donnie announces his resolve to reform, saying that he won't do anything to get sent back to the reformatory (30). He obviously means what he says. Donnie's presentation to Sue of the wooden hors d'oeuvres tray he has made her for Christmas is especially touching. He tells her that he has never before given anyone a Christmas gift, and then he embarrassedly thrusts the gift at her (77).

When she is genuinely delighted with the gift, Donnie is incredulous. He is so overpowered by emotion that he has to leave the apartment so that no one will see his tears. Donnie is irresistibly appealing at this point. His audience appeal far exceeds anything that Kenny achieved in *Loss* or that Sonny Flood achieved in *Dark*. His one limitation is that he is not entirely fair in his representation of Bernie to Sue. Audiences, however, could excuse this unfairness because they know the state of Donnie's desperation. His vulnerability makes him all the more appealing.

It is largely because of Donnie's appeal to audiences that his committing murder at the end of the play brought such negative response from critics and playgoers. One might ask whether the Donnie whom audiences see would be capable of committing the crime with which the play ends. Certainly audiences know that Donnie has committed acts of violence before, but the Donnie Inge presents to them seems genuinely reformed.

Donnie has suffered rejection all his life, and this rejection is reemphasized by Sue's distraught outburst against her son immediately before the murder. In the light of his mother's outburst, Donnie's crime *is* credible. The problem is that it creates a dramatically unsatisfactory ending for the play because the author depends upon shock effect and sensation to achieve his conclusion. Artistically and psychologically, the ending is perhaps tenable. Dramatically and commercially, it is not. Audiences reacted in such horror that the ending blotted out the rest of the play and vitiated the earlier dramatic effects Inge built calculatedly and well.

Had the play ended with Donnie's kissing the woman passionately, the same dramatic and artistic ends would have been attained, and audiences would have found the ending more acceptable. Such an ending would have been psychologically like the ending of *Loss*, but by ending the play at the beginning of a passionate romance between Donnie and the woman, Inge would have avoided some of the pitfalls critics objected to in the denouement of *Loss*. Donnie's murder of the woman in *Affection* offers overt evidence of his extreme reaction to his mother's rejection, but Donnie's seduction of this woman could have indicated the same basic resolution.

Like Donnie, Vince Brinkman knows rejection. Claire obviously does not love him, nor is it likely that she will ever find sexual satisfaction with just one man. She is basically immature and her great insecurity makes her require the constant reassurance of a succession of lovers. She needs Vince because she has to have someone in her life who loves her worshipfully, as he does. She feeds parasitically on Vince's love and uses it to overcome her feelings of insecurity and loneliness. Although she loathes Vince and is unable either to love or respect him, she needs him desperately.

Vince showers people with gifts. This is his form of overcompensation. He gives Claire no spending money but buys her lavish presents. He also lavishes gifts on Sue and Bernie. In a sense, he is trying to expiate through gift-giving a guilt that is a manifestation of such a combination of causes that it is impossible to fathom all of them with the limited knowledge of Vince that one derives from the play.

Claire is emotionally a child. She has known little economic security in her early life. The large, luxurious Brinkman apartment becomes a status symbol for her. Claire was the baby of her family and says she wishes she were home with her parents where she would not be lonely (23). Claire and Vince merely intensify each other's loneliness.

Nearly every critic of *Natural Affection* complained about the vulgarity and crudity of Vince's drunk scene. Vince raves on about sex to the point of embarrassment and the audience is greatly relieved when he finally passes out. Inge has presented other sex-starved characters in his plays, but this is the first time he has used such a sexually explicit outburst on the stage. The vulgarity of the dialogue is not unconvincing, but it is of questionable taste and of negligible dramatic necessity. Inge countered the criticism by saying he felt he could best create the atmosphere he was striving for by writing about common people, using the language they use. He rejected critics' allegations that *Affection* was an immoral play (ix).

Playwrights must make difficult choices. When they believe what they write is plausible, they sometimes must stick to their guns and say, "The critics be damned!"—and this is sometimes a wise artistic decision. But playwrights who take this independent stand must realize that it may jeopardize the commercial success of their plays. If they want public acclaim, they sometimes need to adapt their writing to what critical sentiment demands.

Because Inge refused to give in to critics and to audiences who found *Affection* offensive, the play was doomed commercially. Overwhelmed by the failure of the play, he could easily have salvaged the production by modifying the ending and by either toning down or excluding Vince's drunk scene. Conscientious authors do not like to be faced with such decisions when they sincerely believe, as Inge did, that they have written a play that is true to life. Inge found himself in a dilemma, and his refusal to alter *Affection* left him with a play that would not work on Broadway.

Affection nevertheless contains some of Inge's best writing. Gone is the awkward presentation of background material that is sometimes a problem in his other, more successful plays. With admirable subtlety, he provides audiences with the insights and information they need to understand the play. He is graceful in letting the audience know that Donnie can stay home permanently if his mother will agree. The audience knows this significant fact before Sue does. Sue relates Donnie's history to Bernie the morning of Donnie's arrival, and it is natural that she should do so because Bernie, who does not know Donnie, needs to receive the same information the audience requires. Donnie's arrival in an empty apartment with his companion, Gil, gives Inge another opportunity to inform the audience about necessary details.

Most of the speeches in the play are clipped and realistic. The natural, free-flowing dialogue proceeds at a better pace than the dialogue did in his earlier plays, where some monotonous fits of introspection overtook the characters at times, and tiresome soliloquies resulted. In *Affection,* the dialogue is crisp and convincing. The only fits of introspection occur when Claire and Vince examine their situation in act 2 and when Sue becomes reminiscent in act 7. In both instances, these lines pass quickly and are motivated by a significant cause—Vince's drunkenness and Claire's insecurity or Sue's guilt at not having been able to give Donnie the attention mothers are expected to give their offspring.

Inge's setting emphasizes skillfully and with ironic effect the dreariness of the climate as opposed to the forced gaiety of the holiday season. The Christmas season is integral to the play, because Donnie is released from the work farm to celebrate it. Sue's jealousy of Claire is partly attributable to Claire's taking advantage of the spirit of the season and being more free than she might otherwise have been in kissing Bernie. Vince's intoxication early in the evening is more convincing on Christmas Eve than it might have been on an ordinary day. The general sentiment of the mother-son relationship is made more poignant by the season and all it implies.

When he wrote about the play in the *New York Times,* Howard Taubman commented on Inge's passage in *Affection* in which Claire comments on Williams's *Sweet Bird of Youth* asking how shows like that are permitted. She thinks Williams's characters are sick and doesn't understand why playwrights cannot write plays about respectable people. She doesn't know where Williams finds characters like those he writes about (82). It is ironic that Claire, the most Williams-like character in the play should have this speech.

Of the allusion to Williams, Taubman writes, "One of Mr. Inge's characters, in an outburst of discontent with the world as it is, demands to know why Mr. Williams writes with such violence about such sick people. Before the play is finished, the joke becomes savagely ironic. For 'Natural Affection' . . . is about people whose emotional and psychic health is anything but certifiable."[16] The irony of Claire's speech, of course, pervades the play. It heightens the idea that people are not able to see themselves in perspective, and it also prepares the audience for Sue's ultimate decision, a result of her animal nature overcoming her human nature with the result that Donnie will have to return to the work farm.

Audiences might have been happier with the play had Inge allowed it to reach a happy resolution in which Bernie, going along with the spirit of the season, agrees to let Donnie stay with Sue and him. But to do so would have been to give the play a saccharine ending at best. It would also have been an utter impossibility because Donnie demands to have Sue to himself on his own terms. Donnie does nothing to make Bernie like or even tolerate him, although he expresses apprehension about how Bernie will react to him.

In *Affection,* Inge explores the nature of love, and each relationship in the play deals with this concern. Sex is in some way a part of every love relationship in the play, including Donnie's relationship with his mother. Everyone in the drama searches frantically for love, but the obstacles to it always seem greater than the emotion. When Vince comes home early on Christmas morning with some drunks he has picked up, the woman who is hugging her young man asks him to tell her he loves her. He does so instantly but only so that he can haul her off to bed (106). His blatantly insincere expression of love holds a mirror to all the love shown in the play: love is a living arrangement and a sexual accommodation, little more. Yet Sue, faced with a difficult choice, cannot give up what she and Bernie have in favor of the natural affection between mother and son.

Affection was well performed. Kim Stanley was striking as Sue Barker. The supporting cast, which included Henry Guardino as Bernie, Tom Bosley as Vince, Monica May as Claire, and Gregory Rozakis as Donnie, received vociferous acclaim. Tony Richardson directed. Norman Nadel of the *New York World-Telegram* wrote of *Affection,* "American playwright William Inge and English director Tony Richardson are a powerful new pair in the theater. For proof of this you need look no further than 'Natural Affection,' newly arrived at the Booth. The problem is that these two established artists don't know how to control that power." Nadel then accuses Inge and Richardson of being possessed of "eagerness to produce the dirtiest play of the year." Nadel identifies sex as the play's central theme and contends that "the exploration of several complex and troubled characters becomes only the accessory."[17]

The Broadway production gave this impression more than a reading of the play does, and the direction emphasized sexuality and made the crucial murder scene at the end an overtly sexual act. The repeated introduction of Donnie's twist recording implies that a basic sexuality underlies much of the play. It is significant that Donnie plays the record immediately after he has committed murder.

Commenting on the sensationalism, Richard Watts wrote in the *New York Post* that apparently Inge "decided it was the qualities of sensationalism in the work of Williams and Albee that gave them their excellence and [he] set out to beat them at their own game." This assessment seems simplistic. Watts, however, is justified in concluding that "the fact proved in 'Natural Affection' is that the sensationally lurid is not Mr. Inge's field. Instead of seeming an integral part of his work, it appears to be clumsily imposed, and, in the process of trying it, his splendid capacity for compassion and human understanding slowly disappear, and a kind of extravagant foolishness and ineptness is substituted."[18]

Although there is some validity to Watts's conclusions, one wonders why there was so much objection to *Affection's* sensationalism when there was no real objection to the same basic kind of sensationalism in *Splendor*. In this script, Ace Stamper commits suicide, Deanie lands in a mental institution, and prostitutes figure in the latter part of the action. The answer to this question probably is that in *Splendor* the sensationalism is presented more gradually, is built up to more effectively than it was in *Affection*. The murder in this play shocked audiences in much the way Sammie's suicide did in *Dark,* but is even more intense because it happens onstage.

The appearance of the woman, her attempted seduction of Donnie, and his murder of her are so unanticipated that they explode upon the spectator with the violence of a tornado. Like Doc's drunk scene in *Sheba,* the murder scene becomes a sudden frenzy of activity. In *Affection,* however, the play ends with this shocking scene, so the opportunity for the sort of resolution one finds in *Sheba* and in *Dark* is foreclosed. The playgoers have consistently been led to identify with Donnie, and Inge suddenly pulls the rug out from under them. They leave the theater, quite understandably, in a state of shock.

Artistically, it is hard to view *Affection* as a failure. It might have been a commercial success had slight revisions toned down the ending and had someone with the restraint of Harold Clurman been charged with the direction. This play is the first major production in which Inge has avoided the utter banality and drabness that one finds in the bulk of his characters in all the full-length plays.

Where's Daddy?

In the summer of 1965, Inge went east to work on the summer tryout of his new play, *Family Things.*[19] The play, his first comedy, toured New England and, according to Inge, "had been playing very successful previews for six weeks."[20] He continues, "We [the cast and crew] began to take ourselves for granted." The play, retitled *Where's Daddy?,* opened in New York at the Billy Rose Theater on 2 March 1966 and closed after twenty-one performances.

Shortly before the opening, Betty Field, who played Mrs. Bigelow, developed laryngitis, which delayed the opening for three days. Inge recalls that "after she came back, nothing seemed to work. Everything was out of joint. The laughs didn't come and it was just heart-breaking."[21] Despite some extremely good lines and despite Inge's excellent portrayal of both Mrs. Bigelow and Professor Pinkerton (Pinky), a professor of English played by Hiram Sherman, the play came across neither as the comedy Inge had intended nor as a credible statement of the social comment it struggled to make.

The play's set is simple. The entire action takes place over an eighteen-hour period in a cold-water flat in New York City. The apartment, after months of habitation, is still filled with packing cases and does not look inhabited.[22] Teena, played on Broadway by Barbara Dana, and Tom Keen, played on Broadway by Beau Bridges, occupy the flat. They have been married a short time. Tom has insisted upon this marriage so that the child they have conceived will be legitimate. The improbable prenuptial agreement he and Teena have reached is that as soon as the baby is born, it will be put up for adoption and the parents will divorce. Tom, who wants to be an actor and has begun to have some success making commercials, has agreed to pay Teena's hospital bills. The two appear to have a friendly and caring relationship, although both are immature. Like Kenny and Lila in *Loss,* they seem to be playing house.

Tom's insistence upon marrying Teena and making their child respectable is explained somewhat by his comment that his own birth was never legally recorded (47). Tom's orthodox morality reminds one of Bo's naive insistence in *Bus Stop* that Cherie marry him because he has been familiar with her. In both cases, the male is cast in the unique role of insisting upon a conventional outcome following sexual dalliance.

Neither Tom nor Teena has had a conventional upbringing. The audience learns little about Tom's earliest years, except that he spent them in an orphanage, much as Donnie did in *Affection*. By the time he was fifteen, however, Tom was hustling in a gay bar where Pinky picked him up. Pinky subsequently provided Tom with a home to which Tom now wants to return. Pinky discourages this, realizing that Tom must face his responsibilities. He reminds Tom that he is about to become a father, which means that he must grow up, a step that some men never take, thereby robbing themselves of their dignity (43). Pinky urges Tom to accept his role as husband and father. If the implication is that the acceptance of this role will bring Tom a new dignity and bearing, nothing in the action of the play suggests that such will be the case.

Teena is the only child of a couple who had been married for twenty-four years before Teena's birth. Mrs. Bigelow became a mother at forty-six. They live in Andover, Massachusetts, and Mrs. Bigelow fancies herself to be a liberal, although it quickly becomes apparent that she is a middle-class WASP who does not understand the term. She has never really had her liberality put to the test, although some of the events in the play come close to testing it: Tom and Teena's plan to put the child up for adoption and divorce each other, the fact that Teena's neighbors and close friends are black, and the realization that Tom has been brought up by a homosexual. Early in the play Mrs. Bigelow reveals the kind of liberal she is when she proclaims that she is not shocked and goes on to say that it doesn't do any good nowadays to be shocked by anything (11). If Mrs. Bigelow is a liberal, she is a liberal by default rather than conviction.

The two other principals in the six-member cast are Helen, played in the original production by Barbara Ann Teer, and Razz, played by Robert Hooks. The two live together down the hall from Tom and Teena and are their friends. Helen and Razz provide Inge with the opportunity to depict Mrs. Bigelow as she really is. They are the first blacks to appear in any of Inge's major writing, perhaps indicative of the impact the Civil Rights movement of the 1960s was having on Inge, who is later (in his novel, *Good Luck, Miss Wyckoff*) to give Miss Wyckoff a black lover.

Helen and Razz are certainly not radical blacks. Razz wants to be an actor and many of his lines in act 2 are recitations from Shakespeare. Helen wishes that she and Razz could marry and have children, but Razz feels it would not be practical for them to do so. They are good and dependable neighbors who see Teena through the birth of her child, who summon the doctor and Mrs. Bigelow to Teena's bedside when she is having the baby, and who give general counsel. In a way, Inge seems to be saying that blacks, like homosexuals, are pretty much like other people.

Inge understands perfectly Mrs. Bigelow's knee-jerk liberalism, and it is agonizing to hear her wonderful lines and those of Pinky, yet to realize that the focus of the play is on Tom and Teena, whose lines are vapid by comparison. At one point, Mrs. Bigelow tells Razz, after having gratuitously expressed her approval of Marian Anderson, that she has never had the opportunity to meet "one of you" socially. She explains awkwardly that she and her husband do not go out much and goes on to say that she met a very nice Negro lady on the P. T. A. board at one of Teena's schools and that she had once had tea with her (89). Mrs. Bigelow has been so racially insulated that she does not realize how offensive this speech is and regards it instead as a genuine demonstration of her openness in racial matters. In the course of this exchange, Razz's responses are clipped and diabolically amusing. Mrs. Bigelow finally admits to feeling comfortable with him, and he responds lacklusterly, "That's good" (90). Razz knows the Mrs. Bigelows of this world and knows how to cope with them. His answers demonstrate that he feels a sense of his own superiority over them. Inge reveals his excellent insight into the upper-middle-class, WASP mindset in the exchanges between Razz and Mrs. Bigelow.

Pinky is the most amusing character in the play and certainly has the best lines. He fits the Inge stereotype of a professor, taking time to correct Tom's usage and punctuation in a letter Tom has written him before he begins to discuss the crucial situation regarding Teena's pregnancy that was the central concern of that letter. Like a good English professor he cites his sources and is even liberal enough to allow that, according to Fowler, "none" as subject can take a plural verb, but expresses his preference for the purist usage, "none is."

Inge's professor stereotype appears earlier in both *Bus Stop* and in his one-act play *Strains of Triumph,* in which Professor Lyman and Professor Benoit, respectively, are each unmarried during the action of the play—Lyman has been married and divorced three times—and suffer from complexes that make them different from most men. Lyman has an unnatural affinity for young girls; Benoit apparently has a Madonna complex, perhaps a mask for the latent homosexual leanings that are suggested by the fact that he likes to sit on the hill and watch scantily clothed young men run the relays. Neither Lyman nor Benoit is really a participant in life, and this appears to be Inge's view of professors, a passive lot of people who make no real contributions to society.

One might ask whether Inge's portrayal of professors is motivated more by his view of professors or by his view of himself as a professor. Although he apparently gave sensitive critiques of the writing his more promising students submitted to him, Kathrene Casebolt, who knew Inge well during his six years in St. Louis, recalls that "Bill was not an illuminating teacher. He would say, 'Well, write what you want to.' "[23] During his early days in teaching, especially during his time at Washington University, Inge did not want to be teaching. His consuming interest was in writing, from which teaching distracted him. Robert Cohen, his colleague at the University of California at Riverside, where Inge taught irregularly in his last years, recalls, "while Inge was very interested in his students and their work, he had no pedagogical technique and was very uncritical in judging student work . . . he often did not feel equal, in some way, to meeting his classes and would frequently and at the last minute ask to be excused from teaching for a given quarter."[24] Inge wrote of professors, perhaps, as he wrote of homosexuals, using his characters to vindicate himself rather than to try to reach generalizations about a group.

In *Daddy,* Pinky is clearly homosexual, as was Vince in *Affection.* Inge's plays of the 1960s deal openly with homosexuality, whereas his plays of the 1950s could not. Charles Burgess speculates, "To hold the teaching and newspaper jobs Inge had before going to New York, any homosexual inclinations probably were severely repressed. . . . Inge's plays in the 1960s presented homosexuals in major roles to an audience conditioned by that decade to accept such stage characters."[25] Not only had the times changed to the point that Inge could now be more open about homosexuality than he was in the past, but the psychoanalysis he had been through by this time helped him to understand human sexuality, particularly homosexuality, better than he had a decade earlier.

Pinky is more overtly homosexual than any other Inge character. Tom, the ex-hustler who is devoted to Pinky, questions his own sexual orientation, asking at one point whether he might really be homosexual and unable to admit it (55). Certainly Tom's gratitude to Pinky is sincere. Pinky comes closer to being a parent for Tom than anyone he has ever known, and Tom loves Pinky as he would love a father. Pinky has helped Tom make something of himself and, presumably, has not made sexual demands upon him. Pinky is the personification of a formal and conventional morality. When Tom reminds him that he was not on a welfare mission to the gay bar in which the two met, Pinky rebukes him and justifies his own actions by saying archly that *he* was not fifteen and that he did have the decency to be shocked when he learned how old Tom was (36).

Pinky makes it clear that he does not want Tom to come back to live with him, so Tom does not have an easy out when he is faced with the prospect of leaving his nineteen-year-old wife. Tom is far from affluent, and he has agreed to send Teena money after he leaves. He has counted on being able to return to live with Pinky until he is better able to provide for himself.

Teena's parents are willing to help their daughter financially, but she wants to be independent of them. She loves Tom, and she immediately comes to love the baby she bears him. Tom does not want to see the baby, but when Teena suddenly delivers two weeks early, Tom sees his son. Teena tells him she is not going to give the baby away. Tom accuses her of defying him, of not following through on their agreement, but Teena is resolute about keeping their child.

Tom, with help from Razz and Pinky, who give Tom a couple of stiff drinks, finally breaks down in tears at the awesome realization that he is a father. As the play ends, Tom—whose analyst now rejects him—and Teena are going to stay together and raise their child. Mrs. Bigelow, who needs to be needed, is going to help, as will Pinky, who will now presumably begin to knit baby clothes rather than sweaters for his poodle.

The basic problem with *Daddy* is that its two leading characters are boorish children who talk in the Freudian jargon they have picked up during their respective analyses—Teena was earlier institutionalized for a breakdown—and who have a preposterously unrealistic view of their situation. Teena tells Mrs. Bigelow, her mother, who has come to help her, that she and Tom are both trying to overcome their backgrounds and have rejected what the Bigelows stand for. She claims that they are trying to live by the highest modern principles (17–18). If this is the reason they have elected to abrogate responsibility for the child they have conceived, their moral values are indeed questionable, as is Teena's judgment in suggesting that her parents' principles are not up to her own.

Tom later in the play expresses his wish that the fetus had been aborted, but Teena was three months pregnant by the time they got around to discussing the matter, and to abort the fetus that late would have imperiled the mother's life. Tom reluctantly allows that he is glad *he* was not flushed down the drain as an unwanted fetus, which, in view of his background, might well have happened.

It is obvious in the play that Inge has several axes to grind, and, as the *New Republic* reviewer notes, he uses the play as a vehicle for expressing himself on a number of topics ranging from teenage dress to avant-garde drama.[26] In doing so, he loses the impact of what he really needs to be writing about. The play has an even greater problem in that the secondary characters, Pinky and Mrs. Bigelow, and to a slighter extent, Helen and Razz, are much more sympathetic and appealing than the main characters.

In the character of Pinky, Inge is clearly trying to present the concerned, socially contributing homosexual. In essence, Pinky is Inge's attempt at self-justification for the homosexuality that he never fully accepted in himself. Although he could come to grips with his homosexuality on an intellectual level, he failed to accept it at the emotional level. Kathrene Casebolt recalls that Inge "didn't approve of himself . . . in his own mind he was truly not at peace."[27] It is doubtful that Inge ever gained peace with himself.

In his attempt at self-justification, Inge sets Pinky up as the paragon who, despite his homosexuality, espouses conventional points of view. He tells Mrs. Bigelow that he still believes in God and love and the family, which he identifies as values that are now considered reactionary

(95). Pinky is on the one hand a caricature of the college professor, about whom Inge had ambivalent feelings, and on the other hand the spokesman for an attitude that takes a jaundiced view of today's youth, of today's theater, of method acting, and of modern psychology.

Pinky is Inge's attempt to show that homosexuals are pretty much like other people, except for their one notable difference. He is basically an honorable person who has not only rescued Tom from a hopeless adolescence, but who has earned Tom's enduring affection, as is evidenced by Tom's admitting that he was lucky that Pinky took him in (37).

Inge would have had a better play had he written it strictly from the viewpoints of Pinky and Mrs. Bigelow because these were the characters with whom he could most convincingly identify. Had *Sheba* been written from the points of view of Marie and Turk, it would have been a much different play, and probably not a successful one. The play succeeded because Inge created convincing major characters in his portrayals of Lola and Doc, and they were convincing because Inge could write from inside their psyches, which he could not do when he wrote about Tom and Teena.

Speaking of Inge's first four plays, Morris Freedman wrote, "William Inge's husbands, wives, and children are far less abrasive than Edward Albee's or Tennessee Williams's families. Inge has 'delighted' more audiences than Albee and Williams."[28] In his three succeeding plays, however, Inge failed to delight audiences in the way Freedman speaks of. In *Daddy,* such is particularly the case. One finds little in the play to sympathize with, except, perhaps, for the poor innocent baby who is being born into a situation that offers little promise. The play's resolution comes about without any perceptible changes in the two protagonists, at least not of the sort that would make one believe they will be capable of providing their child with what is best for it or, indeed, that they will likely hold together as a family for very long.

Intended as a comedy, *Daddy,* although it has its comic moments and although it has some extremely witty lines, does not come across as the kind of comedy that Neil Simon was beginning to provide in *Barefoot in the Park* (1964). The play has many of the elements of the Simon comedy—the run-down apartment, the Bohemian younger generation, the matronly mother, the comic older male figure—but the fact that Tom and Teena have reached the agreement they have about the baby imposes a social concern that prevents *Daddy* from being the comedy it might have been. Instead, the play at times approaches melodrama, particularly in the exchanges between Tom and Teena.

The neat resolution reminds one of television soap operas. It is an unsatisfying and oversimplified solution to the problem Inge has presented. The closing action when the now-domesticated Tom takes the baby's bottle from the stove and tests the temperature of its contents on his wrist is too sweet. What has happened to the high principles of which Teena spoke earlier? What has become of the philosophy that she and Tom worked through as they moved toward their decision about what to do with the baby?

The ending actually is not much different from the endings in most Inge plays: two people face the reality of having to make a compromise to keep from being alone. However, in the first four plays, this ending was approached convincingly. As each of the earlier plays evolved, the options available to the principals narrowed until finally the only reasonable and acceptable option was to accept the compromise that living together entailed.

Doc and Lola, Rosemary and Howard, Cora and Rubin had all pretty much exhausted their options by the time the play ended. None had very glamorous or even hopeful futures to contemplate. They had to decide whether to spend the rest of their lives alone or with someone they had already grown used to. Bo and Cherie do not quite fall into the same category as the others because Bo seemingly has a future on his farm in Montana. Cherie, however, has about exhausted her options, and she makes a practical decision when she goes off with Bo at the end of *Bus Stop*.

Tom and Teena are in quite different circumstances. Tom presumably has a reasonable career ahead of him making commercials and possibly acting. He is young, vibrant, and good-looking. Teena at nineteen has the support of her family should she need it. The future is before her. She might well make something of herself. She does not face the bleak future of Lola or Rosemary or Cora Flood, none of whom has much alternative to the solution she finally accepts.

However, in true Inge style, Teena, who is shown when the curtain rises as a caring, domestic creature, washing Tom's socks and giving him instructions on how to wash them after he leaves and they divorce, finally has her way. She obviously does not want to lose Tom, but she wants him on her own terms. As the play ends, Teena has tamed Tom, as Inge's women always tame their men. Pinky has suggested that, in becoming a father, Tom will discover his manhood. The final implication of the play seems more accurately to be that, by becoming a husband, Tom will be domesticated. Given the immaturity of both Tom and

Teena, however, one must question seriously whether they have any future together.

The critics tore into *Daddy* more viciously than they had torn into any previous Inge play. What Henry Hewes wrote in *Saturday Review* perhaps explains better than any other review why the critical reception was so violently negative: "Mr. Inge's greater talent makes his lapses more lamentable."[29] Hewes felt that the play would have succeeded better as an absurdist drama than as a slice-of-life domestic drama, although this suggestion is hard to take seriously. Inge was crushed by what he considered the vindictiveness of the reviews, and *Where's Daddy?* was to be his last major Broadway play, although another of his plays, *The Last Pad,* was produced off-Broadway in 1970.

The Later Plays

Walter Kerr bemoaned the passing of the William Inge who wrote *Dark.* He called the play "a touching example of one of our commonest theatre experiences: the memory play." He went on to say, "If Mr. Inge's mood had most often been rueful, it had always been warm. If the voices overheard in parlors and bars had always had a commonplace twang to them, their very commonness and familiarity had helped to stir our affection."

Kerr complains that *Loss* was "neither familiar in spirit nor touching in effect," and he blames this not on the playwright's momentary fatigue, but on a tendency in American theater for "the dramatist to work in an ever narrower range, and with an ever softer and more indulgent touch."[30] What Kerr says, of course, is nothing new. Critics through the years had objected to Inge's narrow range and had lamented his concentration on the same basic type of characters in all his plays. His range seems no narrower in *Loss* than it was in his earlier plays, and certainly *Affection* and *Daddy* both broadened the range somewhat, but with catastrophic results. If Inge had been blamed earlier for being a violin with one string, he was now thoroughly castigated for trying to live down that assessment.

Loss and *Daddy* were demonstrably weak in focus, as numerous critics noted. *Affection,* on the other hand, has significant strengths that no previous Inge production had. Criticism of the play often was based on moral objections rather than on artistic ones. Such judgments have always been made of naturalistic and realistic literature, but most have been patently unjust. Accurate depiction is the basic requisite of such literature, and such depiction necessarily offends some audiences and some critics.

One critic wrote, "The real weakness of [*Affection* is] the application of extreme realism to a group of people profoundly unreal."[31] This statement is unsupported in the review and simply is not justifiable. The principals in both the main plot and the subplot are well conceived and are impelled by valid psychological motives. The characters are well developed in terms both of their backgrounds and of their reactions to the immediate situations in which Inge places them.

Inge's characters, particularly in the last three Broadway plays, are not always easy to accept. They are not necessarily pleasing as human beings. But the playwright obviously is under no obligation to create *pleasing* characters; the only artistic requisite is that they be convincing. In most cases, Inge's characters are real.

In the preface to *Affection* (ix), Inge acknowledges that the play may offend the sensibilities of audiences. He admits that he has similar sensibilities, and that these sensibilities made it difficult for him to write the play. Inge suggests here the crux of the problem with this play, and certainly what he says can be applied with equal validity to his two other plays of this period.

There is a degree of truth in John McCarten's suggestion that Inge "set himself up as a junior-varsity Tennessee Williams"[32] when he wrote *Affection*. Violence like Donnie's did not pervade Inge's earlier writing, whereas it had been prevalent in a number of Williams's early plays. The shocking conclusion of *Affection* represents Inge trying to be Williams rather than Inge being Inge. The play's ending failed so badly that, unfortunately, it colored critical assessments of the play as a whole.

Inge's scenario, *Splendor,* avoids the slickness that characterizes considerable scriptwriting. The scenario has great fluidity, and the medium for which Inge was writing permitted him to experiment with a broader approach to his work than he had previously tried. Writing scenarios afforded Inge an artistic freedom that the stage did not.

Splendor would have been a stronger script had the conclusion followed the climax more closely than it did. The wrap-up scenes employ the Dickensian device of showing how the story worked out in the end, a method that seems contrived and unnecessary in modern drama. Ace Stamper's suicide marks the dramatic end of the film, and it is at this point or shortly after it that the film should have ended.

What do the three plays and the scenario considered in this chapter suggest about William Inge? Certainly the scenario suggests that Inge might have had a more illustrious career in scriptwriting had he pursued it. The three plays suggest that Inge tried too hard to answer the critics who accused him of having a limited range. *Bus Stop* should have disabused them of such a notion. However, as Inge's involvement in his own psychoanalysis progressed, his writing sometimes dealt with characters and situations that were not really from his own heart or background.

Perhaps Inge was a fiddle with one string, but that one string was an umbilical cord to the heartland, and it was when Inge stopped writing about the heartland and its simple, small-town people that his plays appealed less to audiences who judged his new work not just on the basis of what it was but also on the basis of how it compared to what they had come to expect of him.

Certainly the excruciating failure of *Daddy* marked the end of Inge's Broadway career and, to an extent, of his career as an artist. The couple of short plays that followed and the two published novels did not enable him to reestablish his reputation of the 1950s. He came inevitably to view himself as a writer who could no longer write. True or false, this self-judgment was paralyzing to a sensitive man who lived to write, who wanted to do nothing else with his life. In the final six years of his life, Inge's reason for being ceased. Left with the conviction that only one course was open to him, he took that course: suicide.

Chapter Four
The Shorter Plays

"All people are divided into two groups, those who participate and those who watch and observe."
—From *The Strains of Triumph*

William Inge's shorter plays are revealing because they often serve as notebooks for recording materials that recur in the longer plays or that suggest his intellectual and psychological interests at the time. These plays experiment with different locales from those of Inge's first four Broadway productions. Although two of his last Broadway plays were set in Chicago and one was set in New York, most of his early Broadway plays were set in small towns in Oklahoma or Kansas during the 1920s or 1930s. A number of the short plays are set in such locales as a mining town near Pittsburgh (*The Boy in the Basement*), New York (*To Bobolink, For Her Spirit* and *An Incident at the Standish Arms*), Southern California (*A Social Event*), and an unidentified seaside resort (*Memory of Summer* and *The Mall*).

Five of the shorter plays might have taken place anywhere—*The Rainy Afternoon*, *The Strains of Triumph*, *The Disposal*, *The Last Pad*, and *The Tiny Closet*. The directions in the last three say they are set in the Midwest, although nothing in the plays necessitates this locale. *Bus Riley's Back in Town* is set in Texas, but another version of the play, *Glory in the Flower*, seems to be set in the Kansas or Oklahoma with which Inge was most familiar.

Variety of locale is, of course, not the chief characteristic that distinguishes the short plays from the longer ones. Taken as a group, the shorter plays deal largely with a broad variety of classical psychological disorders, all of which became increasingly interesting to Inge as his own psychoanalysis progressed. At times Inge writes virtual case studies of people with various psychological conditions and uses these conditions as the focus for his short plays.

Inge wrote the shorter plays collected in *Summer Brave and Eleven Short Plays* between 1949 and 1957. He did the earliest of these, *To Bobolink, For Her Spirit*, in his last months in St. Louis just before he left Washington University and went to New York to see *Sheba* into production. Characters who appear or are mentioned in the shorter plays reappear in some of Inge's longer work. Del Loomis from *Splendor* is first mentioned in *Bus Riley's Back in Town,* although he never actually appears in the shorter play. Joker Evans, the delivery boy from the supermarket in *The Boy in the Basement,* reappears as the same general sort of character in *Glory in the Flower,* although the circumstances of his presentation in the later play are different from those in the earlier one.

Bus Riley reminds one of Hal in *Picnic* as Inge presents him in *Bus Riley's Back in Town* and of Ace Stamper in *Splendor* as Inge presents him in *Glory in the Flower.* Viola in *Memory of Summer* closely resembles Lila in *Loss.* Inge's garrulous women—Lola in *Sheba* and Lottie in *Dark,* for example—are found in the shorter plays in characters like Mrs. Scranton in *The Boy in the Basement* and Mrs. Crosby in *The Tiny Closet.*

The shorter plays often seem to be exercises that gave Inge the opportunity to work out characterizations he was shaping. He claimed that a number of his shorter plays were fragments he wrote to explore characters he might use in his later work.[1]

To Bobolink, For Her Spirit

Bobolink Bowen, fat and fiftyish, hair kinky, eyes reduced to slits by the strong corrective lenses she has to wear, is as unlikely a protagonist as one can ask for. Inge, who understands the psychology of such people, however, presents her with warmth and respect. Writing this short play at about the time he was writing *Sheba,* Inge envisioned Shirley Booth as Bobolink. The character bears a general resemblance to Lola Delaney.

Inge refuses to sentimentalize Bobolink, but rather draws her with artistic detachment. Bobolink lives an existence that would seem meaningless to many people. The high point in her life is to haunt the sidewalk outside the 21 Club in New York to collect the autographs of the famous people who patronize the club. Bobolink has seniority among the other autograph collectors who huddle on the sidewalk with her. Within her narrow context, she is preeminent. Her fellow autograph collectors regard her as the final authority and arbiter in matters connected with stage and screen personalities.

Inge had a childhood fascination with film stars. As he was growing up, Inge, like Sonny in *Dark,* collected the stars' photographs much as Bobolink collects their autographs. This awe of actors is shown in *Loss* when a wide-eyed Kenny tells Lila that he has never known an actress. In *Bus Stop,* Elma is dazzled when she learns that Cherie has worked in a nightclub.

Bobolink is little more than a vignette in which Inge presents a woman whose life would be completely empty were it not for her autograph collecting. If Bobolink seems a sad figure, it is because the audience would not like that life for themselves. Inge presents her neutrally. He allows her the pride she has in being the best of the autograph collectors and, within the circumscribed world he creates for her, Inge permits Bobolink to have dignity.

In one memorable scene, Bobolink declines to ask for autographs from two well-dressed, beautiful people exiting from 21. A fellow collector, Anna-Marie, asks them to sign her book, thinking they might be famous someday. Bobolink, however, is too venerable in her avocation to waste her time on those who are not yet famous (126).

Although Inge's material here would have lent itself well to satire, he was not comfortable satirizing common people. He had too much respect for humans to do that. Rather, in *Bobolink,* he presents a brief slice-of-life, a play with no defined beginning or ending, just an event, a middle that he never worked into the full-blown play it was probably too insubstantial to become. If the play has any theme, it is that one should accept one's lot as gracefully as possible, which is exactly what Bobolink has done. If Bobolink has agonizing moments of loneliness and uncertainty, if she is disturbed by the futility of her life, Inge does not note it. Instead he flicks the shutter of his camera and captures a moment in Bobolink's life, which is the strength of his realism.

A Social Event

A Social Event is Inge's only real satire. The play, written shortly after his first exposure to the theatrical worlds of New York and Hollywood, grew out of his perceptions about the phoniness of Hollywood and reminds one of such satires as Clifford Odets's *The Big Knife* (1948) or Nathanael West's *The Day of the Locust* (1939).

As the play opens, Randy and Carole Brooks, an actor and actress, waken in their ostentatious bedroom. They are distraught because they have not been invited to a social event that is to occur at noon, in this case, the funeral of Scotty Woodrow, a well-known actor to whom Hollywood columnists have compared Randy. To make matters worse, Carole has accepted an invitation to a post-funeral gathering being given by Sandra, another actress (154).

Although Randy and Carole never knew Scotty, Randy has been magnanimous in his public utterances about the actor, and such magnanimity, according to Randy's code of etiquette, should be reciprocated by an invitation to the star's funeral. Randy and Carole speak of crashing the funeral, but that would be too demeaning even for them. At the eleventh hour, they try unsuccessfully to get their agent to wangle an invitation for them. Then they consider giving themselves food poisoning so that they can say they were too ill to go.

Just when it seems that no solution is possible, Muriel, their maid, arrives with their breakfast tray and reminds them that she is taking the rest of the day off. It turns out that she has been invited to Mr. Woodrow's funeral because her mother used to work for Scotty. Muriel was born in his beach house. She has also been invited to join the family at their home after the funeral.

Randy immediately asks Muriel whether she has a ride to the funeral. When she says that she hasn't, he volunteers to drive her there. In a wonderfully comic scene, he and Carole scramble to get into their funereal finery so that they won't be late. Carole has the delicious satisfaction of calling Sandra to tell her that they will not be able to attend her post-funeral party because they have to go back to the Woodrow home with some of his closest friends (159).

Although the play is only eight pages long, it is a much more fully realized play than *Bobolink*. Unlike *Bobolink*, which is essentially a sketch, *Event* has a definite beginning in which the basic problem is presented with great verbal economy, a well-sustained middle in which the problem is wrestled with, and a clearly defined ending in which the problem is neatly resolved.

The anticlimax, confined to the last eight speeches, highlights the hypocrisy of the principals in two ways. First, Randy ponders whether it will look right for them to be seen at the funeral with their maid. He concludes, though, that it will not be amiss because funerals are democratic affairs (159). Then Carole makes her haughty telephone call to Sandra asking to be excused from the invitation she earlier accepted.

Event is Inge's most atypical play in setting, characterization, and philosophical approach. His usual realism is underplayed, and his sense of whimsy is more highly developed here than in any of his other work. The play implies that everyone is living a lie, and that their lying makes them suspicious of everyone else. The only shreds of sincerity in the play are those the principals reveal when they try to promote their own careers.

The Boy in the Basement

Certainly the most deeply felt and psychologically complicated of Inge's shorter plays is *The Boy in the Basement*. Spencer Scranton, the protagonist, is a middle-aged, homosexual undertaker who lives with his domineering, self-righteous mother and his deaf, paralyzed father in a small mining town in western Pennsylvania. Spencer's sense of filial duty has robbed him of any chance to have a life of his own.

Spencer's only respite from working with one dead body after another is his weekend jaunts to the nearest large city, Pittsburgh. Mrs. Scranton worries about Spencer's weekends in Pittsburgh, especially after he telephones her in the middle of the night and asks her to wire him two hundred dollars on the pretext of needing to pay for unexpected automobile repairs. When Spencer comes home, she demands to know whether he was with a woman, and when he says he was not, she muses that he has never been interested in women, unlike his brother, whose life was wine, women, and song, and who ended up in a mental institution.

Mrs. Scranton exits to attend a meeting of one of the many civic organizations to which she belongs, and when Spencer tells her to have a good time, she retorts archly that her organizations don't meet so that people can have good times. They meet so that people can accomplish things. It is at this point that Joker Evans, a delivery boy from the supermarket, arrives. He and Spencer have an easy rapport, and Joker is genuinely fond of Spencer.

Joker represents all that Spencer wishes he could be, just as Spencer's father represents what he fears he will become. Joker, young and promising, wants to become a physician. He has won a college scholarship and knows that this is his ticket out of the constricted environment in which he has been raised. He tells Spencer that he has to go to college if he ever hopes to get out of this town.

After Joker leaves, Mrs. Scranton returns prematurely from her meeting, looking as though she had seen a ghost. She has learned that the police raided the Hi-Ho Bar, a gay hangout near Pittsburgh, on the night that Spencer called her to send him money. She has seen matchboxes from that bar in Spencer's pocket. She confronts Spencer with what she has just heard and accuses him of lewd depravity. Her tirade leads Spencer to pack a suitcase and stalk out of the house, vowing never to return. On this dramatic note, the first scene ends.

The second scene takes place early the next morning. Mrs. Scranton has waited up all night for Spencer, who finally returns. He and his mother settle their differences in a scene that is unabashedly oedipal. The directions indicate their desperate need for each other and the deep love that brings them together like lovers (180). Mrs. Scranton tells Spencer how much she loves him, more certainly than she loves her husband because their love is innocent and demands no physical act for its manifestation. She tells him that she would be ready for the embalming room if he ever left her.

Spencer then learns that a body is about to be delivered for embalming and complains that his life is just a procession of dead bodies (181). When the body arrives, Spencer, to his horror, discovers that it is Joker's. Told that Joker has drowned, Spencer can only repeat the boy's name incredulously. He goes into the embalming room and rubs his hand over Joker's chest. Mrs. Scranton calls down suspiciously to ask what Spencer is doing, and he calls back that she would be suspicious if he were down there alone with a stuffed owl. Then, saying ruefully that he wanted Joker to live (165), he severs his main arteries, feeling the pain as though he were inflicting it upon himself.

Mrs. Spencer, contented that she has made her peace with Spencer, sings "Rock of Ages" (184), and, reminding her son that this is to be a cheap funeral, tells him that she is fixing eggs for breakfast. In what has to be one of the most insensitive lines in American drama, showing precisely the sort of brutal woman Mrs. Scranton is, she then tells Spencer that he can eat his meal while Joker is draining (184).

In many ways, Mrs. Scranton is as fully realized a character as Inge ever created. Despite the play's brevity—it is just over twenty pages long—Mrs. Scranton is developed fully as the overbearing, possessive, domineering hypocrite who emasculates her men and turns them into putty. She won't allow her invalid husband to have a drink, and Spencer has to keep liquor in a jar labeled "Embalming Fluid" so that he can sneak his father a drink when the mother is out. Mrs. Scranton equates pleasure with wickedness and has struggled to keep her body pure, which must certainly have made Mr. Scranton's married life with her a misery. The Victorian house in which the action of the play is set constantly reinforces Mrs. Scranton's Victorian outlook.

Basement is Inge's first play to present a homosexual situation overtly. Spencer's homosexuality precipitates the climax of the first portion of the play, and the audience's knowledge of it makes especially poignant and pathetic the second climax, the death of Joker Evans, whom Spencer loves, even though he is too honorable—or perhaps too frightened—to introduce Joker to gay experience.

Just as Sheba in Inge's first major play represents lost innocence, Joker in this play represents the promise of freedom. Joker realized the necessity of breaking away, but his hope died with him. There certainly is no reasonable hope for Spencer, whose mother, having gained the upper hand decisively, systematically reduces him to a nonentity.

The psychological insights in *Basement* are as sharp as any Inge has presented. It is obvious that he understands the materials with which he is working in this play. Because of the depth of his understanding and because of his close identification with his materials, the play is warm and extremely moving. It is regrettable that Inge never worked these materials into a major play because *Basement* contains some of his finest depiction of character.

The Tiny Closet

Mr. Newbold's name belies his personality. A meticulous man who has lived most of his adult life in rooming houses, Mr. Newbold is a floorwalker in a department store. The audience is told nothing about his past, little about his present, and receives minimal information upon which to speculate about his future. The action of the play is carefully contained within a rooming house over a short period of time.

Mr. Newbold rents a room from Mrs. Crosby, a garrulous woman much concerned with everyone else's business. He insists when he rents the room that he be permitted to install a small lock on the closet in his room. He extracts from Mrs. Crosby a promise that no one will ever go into the closet or seek to discover its contents. Mr. Newbold should have understood human nature well enough to know that making an issue about the closet would insure Mrs. Crosby's finding a way into it at the first opportunity. But Mr. Newbold, an honorable man, expects others to be honorable. He sums up his life neatly when he tells Mrs. Crosby that a closet is a small place and all that he asks for in life is a tiny closet to call his own (190).

Although Mrs. Crosby tells Mr. Newbold that he is her favorite roomer, her model guest, the minute he leaves for work, she calls her friend, Mrs. Hergesheimer, and, after suggesting that Mr. Newbold might be a Communist, gets Mrs. Hergesheimer to come over to help her pick Mr. Newbold's lock, an activity that they have already had a go at earlier. Mrs. Crosby justifies her invasion by citing her fear of Communist infiltration, proclaiming that a schoolteacher who rooms in her house is a Communist even though she goes to church every Sunday.

The two women convince themselves that they have a patriotic duty to get into Mr. Newbold's closet. Just as they penetrate this sanctum, Mr. Newbold, who has grown suspicious of Mrs. Crosby, returns. He is too nervous to go upstairs, and all at once, the two women, who have now achieved their goal and discovered that Mr. Newbold has a closet full of women's hats and sewing equipment, bound down the stairs carrying some of the hats.

Inge chooses not to allow a confrontation between Mr. Newbold and the women, so Mr. Newbold ducks into the hall closet, where he hears the two harpies discussing him accusingly. Mrs. Crosby says she is going to call the department store and tell them what kind of man they have working for them. She tries on one of the elegant hats, and then exits, as Mrs. Hergesheimer already has. Mr. Newbold, bent, shattered, defeated, emerges from the closet, picks up one of the hats lovingly, puts it on, and looks at himself in the mirror. He then falls to the sofa and cries desperately.

In this play, Inge is directly concerned with human dignity and with one's right to privacy. Mrs. Crosby is a surrogate mother in *Closet,* a self-righteous woman much like Mrs. Scranton in *Basement.* Mr. Newbold, timid and lonely, had adjusted to whatever his problem is. The play suggests fetishism, transvestism, and homosexuality, although Inge chooses not to develop these themes overtly. The title also suggests repressed homoerotic tendencies. Were it not for Mr. Newbold's obsession with locking the closet, one might speculate that he moonlights, contrary to company policy, by making hats. The lock on the closet, however, becomes a compelling symbol and suggests that Mr. Newbold keeps most of himself locked up inside.

Closet is played in a minor key, and is perhaps Inge's most restrained play. It succeeds because of its unusually quiet presentation of a highly explosive situation. In none of his other plays does Inge succeed so well in presenting the desperation and clutching loneliness of people. The closet symbolizes Mr. Newbold's only security, with all its return-to-the-womb implications. The security, however, is violated by those who in the name of patriotic duty shatter it.

Written not long after the McCarthy era, the play addresses many of the problems posed by McCarthyism. It does so by stripping bare the soul of a sensitive, harmless man whose quiet conflict with the mores of a hostile, self-righteous, suspicious, and destructive society is exposed and made to look lurid. In *Closet,* Inge makes his most direct statement about individual liberty and freedom of choice.

Memory of Summer

Memory of Summer suggests the atmosphere of both *Sheba* and *Loss.* Viola, the play's central character, is much like Lila in *Loss,* although she lacks Lila's grasp on reality. She is in her forties and has a delicate prettiness. Her husband apparently is a well-to-do businessman from St. Louis. The play finds her at a seaside resort with Alice, her old housekeeper, who is now more nurse-governess than housekeeper.

The play opens as Alice tries to dissuade Viola from going for a swim. The air is cold and swimming is dangerous because it is past Labor Day and no lifeguards are on duty. But Viola is out of touch with reality and does not respond to reason. Alice wants Viola to admit that summer, symbolic of youth, is over, but Viola calls her suggestion nonsense. Alice urges her to pack up and return to St. Louis, but Viola is determined to have her holiday and will not leave.

Viola refuses to admit that her youth is over. In her attempts to prolong her summer, she succeeds only in making herself look foolish. She talks of all the young people she will see at the beach, unwilling or unable to remember they have left. She has romantic dreams of dining at the inn, telling risqué stories to the young people, and dancing with the young men. When Alice reminds her that the young people have left the inn and that the orchestra played its last dance on Labor Day, Viola, pretending not to hear, dashes into the surf.

A young Coast Guardsman blows his whistle at her and shouts that she must come out of the water. Alice runs for a doctor, leaving the Coast Guardsman with a blanket to wrap Viola in and with a flask of brandy he can give Viola to warm her. As soon as Viola emerges from the water, the Coast Guardsman tells her that she cannot swim there any more. Viola's response, a typical Blanche DuBois line, is to tell him that he is gallant to be concerned about her (208). But the Coast Guardsman punctures Viola's romantic balloon by telling her that he is not gallant; he is just following orders.

Memory does not really end; it is more accurate to say that it merely plays out. Viola tries to win the affection of the Coast Guardsman, who rebuffs her. She goes back to the cottage to await the arrival of the doctor Alice has called. At the final curtain, she is still talking about having to look her best for the young people tonight. That the play's conflict is never resolved cannot be regarded as an artistic weakness. It is merely Inge's way of indicating that some situations in life, as unsatisfactory as they may be, merely persist. Inge maintains excellent objectivity in the play. He shows no pity for Viola. Instead, he shows her as she is and leaves it to the audience to react as it will to her.

Bus Riley's Back in Town

Bus Riley's Back in Town opens in the Fiesta Room of the Boomerang Hotel in the middle of Texas, which has recently gone from boom to bust. The bar is all but deserted. Howie, the barkeep, talks with a salesman who remembers how things used to be, how he used to be able to sell five thousand dollars worth of goods in a single day. Now he can just about make expenses.

The two provide necessary background for a play about the reunion of Jackie Loomis and Bus Riley, former lovers who were seventeen and eighteen years old, respectively, when Jackie got pregnant. Her father, Del Loomis, not only forced an abortion upon Jackie, but he also lodged charges against Bus for corrupting the morals of a minor. Bus has not been back in town in the five years since and would not be back now were it not for his father's serious illness. The play could be a continuation of the main action of *Splendor in the Grass,* whose characters and situations parallel those in *Bus Riley.*

Meanwhile, Del Loomis, once the richest man in town, has lost nearly everything and has been chronically ill. Jackie leads a reclusive existence looking after him. She still loves Bus and thinks of him often. But Bus, who now equates love with punishment, has made no effort to see Jackie during his time at home, and he must leave soon.

Jackie goes to the Boomerang to get information about Bus from Howie. She is determined to see Bus while he is home. Her friends Bernice and Ralph try to prevent a reunion, and they drive Jackie back home as soon as Bus, now enlisted in United States Navy, handsome in his uniform, enters the bar. He does not see Jackie.

As soon as Bernice and Ralph, whose chief function is to provide background information, deposit Jackie at home, she gets in her own car and drives back to the Boomerang to have her long-awaited reunion with Bus. All he wants is to get away from the narrow minds and the dust of this little town that he left with such bitterness five years before. Having seen something of the world, Bus realizes that he must get away permanently. This last night at home has filled him with memories, and the strain of his father's illness has left him emotionally pent up.

Bus wants to find some action tonight, and he is talking with Howie and the salesman, the bar's only other customer, about this when Jackie's car pulls up in front. Bus, who has scrupulously avoided talking to Howie and the salesman about her, starts to leave. Howie tries to get him to stay and, in doing so, delays him just long enough that he has to see Jackie.

It quickly becomes clear that no really hard feelings exist between Bus and Jackie themselves. It is just the circumstances of what happened between them that have made Bus bitter. Bus ran head-on into Del Loomis once; he wants to be sure it does not happen again. In Del, Bus was not dealing merely with an outraged father; the play suggests that he was dealing with a man in love with his own daughter.

Before long, Jackie and Bus decide to drive to the next county to get a bottle of liquor. Bus suggests that they stop at Riverview, a roadhouse on the way. Before they leave the Boomerang, Jackie and Bus dance together. Jackie tries to talk about old times, but Bus is unresponsive. The past is too unpleasant for Bus to talk about. He tells Jackie that he doesn't fall in love any more, and later in the play says that love is something one can be jailed for.

By the time Bus makes clear to Jackie that he wants to take her to the Riverview and spend the night with her, he has made it equally clear that *all* he wants is to spend the night with her. He looks for nothing more entangling than a night together. Jackie does not want Bus on such terms, but in the end, she capitulates and goes with him, realizing that if she cannot recapture all of their past together, she can at least recapture the sexual part of it.

The play's ending is probably Inge's most honest ending, unsatisfying though it may be. The suggestion of redemption in the ending of *Sheba* or *Dark* is much less convincing than the meaning this ending conveys. Jackie takes what happiness she can find, making this compromise because something is better than nothing. Inge reinforces the notion that one just has to live life out when he has Bus tell Howie that he will drink his drink up quickly so that Howie can close the bar. But Howie tells him the bar has to stay open whether it has customers or not. This sentiment is consistent with Jackie's having to live life out, to keep open as it were, even though she becomes lonelier and lonelier as she does so.

In *Bus Riley*, Inge shows a greater mastery of his ability to provide necessary background information than in any of his other plays. Howie's conversation with the salesman takes care of a great deal of the business of the play, and Ralph and Bernice also help in this regard. Because Jackie and Bus have been separated from each other for five years, it is also natural for Jackie to provide in her conversations with Bus a great deal of information the audience needs. Both *Bus Stop* and *Loss* would have been stronger plays had Inge been able to use a comparable expository technique in them.

Bus Riley has a few inadequacies. Inge would have done well to make more of Del's relationship with his daughter. Inge also mentions in the play that Bus's mother is Mexican, an unnecessary detail unless he intends to do something with it. The great social irony of the play is that men like Del have built the town up, but that they are now old and dying. Del's past actions were such, however, that Bus, the sort of energetic youth who might bring new life into the town, wants only to leave it and its bitter memories.

Some of the imperfections in *Bus Riley* are absent from *Glory in the Flower*, whose story is essentially the same. This rewritten version of the play, however, is dramatically tighter than the earlier play, as will be seen in the following discussion of it. The Ralph–Bernice sequence is omitted from *Glory*, with the result that the play is more direct and has more dramatic impact than *Bus Riley*. The introduction of new characters and significant changes in the presentation of the principals give the later version increased focus and credibility.

Glory in the Flower

Glory in the Flower contains echoes from a number of other Inge plays, and some of its characters suggest directly characters in other of his plays. The "flower" Inge uses in the title refers to roses that Jackie, now forty and still good-looking, wears in her hair because she thinks they make her look younger than she is. Inge uses them at the end of the play to mark Jackie's finally coming to maturity, as signaled by her snatching them from her hair and throwing them on the floor. In this act, Jackie does essentially what Lola does in *Sheba* when she stops calling the lost dog. Jackie's act suggests the sort of significance Inge attaches to roses in *Loss* as well.

Jackie is a prototype for Lila in *Loss*. The two women are about the same age. Just as Lila has her eyes on Kenny, so does Jackie have designs on a younger man, the eighteen-year-old Joker, who is different in this play from what he is in *Basement*. Now an older woman rather than an older man desires him. But when Jackie finally reaches the point of throwing her flowers away, she can tell Joker that she feels old and is proud of the fact. Whereas Joker is a prime motivating factor in *Basement*, his purpose in *Glory* is to provide contrast. He and his friends provide a mirror to Jackie and Bus's past. Because Inge uses Joker in this way, he can eliminate a great deal of background dialogue about Jackie and Bus.

Glory, like *Bus Riley*, is closely related to *Splendor in the Grass*. In *Glory* Jackie recites the portion from the tenth stanza of William Wordsworth's *Ode on Intimations of Immortality* that contains the words "splendor in the grass." The first version of the romance between Bus Riley and Jackie Loomis is closer to *Grass* than the same romance is in *Glory* because the original version presents Del Loomis as the vengeful parent who interferes with the lives of the two young people. *Glory* omits any reference to Bus's having been jailed on account of Jackie's pregnancy, and the audience is left to think that Bus left town when he realized that a complication had developed in his romance with Jackie.

In *Glory*, Inge presents a Jackie who is not on the prowl for Bus. In this version of the story, Bus has telephoned her. They have agreed to meet at the Paradise Bar. Jackie, who appears on stage before Bus, does not attempt to give the audience any of the details of her past relationship with Bus. Her actions allow the audience to size her up as she is at present. She talks with the younger people, and, according to Inge's directions, acts like a kid herself. She dances with Joker.

The salesman and Howie talk at the bar, as they did in *Bus Riley*, but they tell less than they did in the earlier play. The only hint of background Inge provides before Bus enters is the tantalizing bit when Howie answers the salesman's question about whether Bus is Jackie's husband by saying that he was not ever her husband. The answer leaves the audience with the distinct impression that there is more to be said, but Howie does not say it, nor is he able to because right at that point, Jackie returns from the dance floor. What the audience knows about the situation, it has gleaned from the Jackie-Bus dialogue in the play. Inge shows commendable restraint here, dealing with background material frugally to heighten the play's dramatic effect.

Inge wisely decided in *Glory* to present Jackie and Bus as forty-year-olds rather than as the twenty-three or twenty-four-year-olds they were in *Bus Riley*. Because they are older, their past seems more remote. They are less attached to it than they were in *Bus Riley*. As a result, Bus is not so bitter in *Glory* as he was in *Bus Riley*. When Jackie and Bus meet each other again in *Glory*, they both have established their own lives. Although Jackie leads a dull life as a piano teacher, she has adjusted to her lot. She has had boyfriends, and she has had the opportunity to marry.

Bus lives in California, where he is a small-time boxer and bit actor. Although his account of his life is more glamorous than one can easily believe, it is obvious that he has moved far beyond the small town in which he grew up. Although Jackie and Bus no longer love each other in *Glory*, they have a true sentiment for their mutual past. In *Glory*, Jackie turns down Bus's invitation to spend the night with him. She leaves, then returns to the Paradise just as she returned to the Boomerang in *Bus Riley*, but in this play she returns only to make sure Bus has no hard feelings toward her. He hasn't, so they shake hands and Jackie leaves. This ending, on the whole, is more satisfying than the ending of *Bus Riley*.

Whereas *Bus Riley* was essentially a play about loneliness and continuance, *Glory* is a play about change. Things alter. People grow apart. This is the way life is. In this play, Inge seems to have accepted life on these terms, and the play is strengthened by this acceptance.

The Rainy Afternoon

The Rainy Afternoon is a fragment about childhood. Two young girls, ten-year-old Wilma and seven-year-old Billy Mae, are playing together in an old barn in the Midwest on a rainy afternoon. Dressed up in her mother's dresses and high heels, Wilma soon emerges as an aggressive little brute. Both girls have dolls, and Wilma tells Billie Mae that she is going to spank her doll to make it behave. Billie Mae protests that her doll is behaving, but Wilma forces her to spank the doll and scold it.

The audience soon knows that Wilma has few friends and that those she does have are in her clutches because of her possessiveness. When Billie Mae wants to leave because she is not having fun, Wilma accuses her of not knowing how to play. When ten-year-old Vic Bates appears, however, Wilma immediately relegates Billie Mae to the background. Try as she will, Billie Mae cannot break into the conversation Wilma and Vic are having. After a childhood debate about whether Wilma or Vic's father has the larger car, Wilma decides they should play house. Wilma, of course, will be the mother, Vic the father, and Billie Mae alternately the baby and the maid.

Billie Mae does not want to go along because her mother does not want her to play with boys, but Wilma assures her that what her mother doesn't know won't hurt her. The play proceeds with Hubby arriving home from the office. Wilma tells him that the baby has been very bad today and must be spanked, whereupon Vic spanks Billie Mae, cheered on by Wilma who wants him to spank harder. Billie Mae, understandably, objects to her role in the play, so Wilma sends her to bed. She then reenters the scene as the maid.

As the play progresses, Wilma graduates to the role of enchantress who now tries to get Hubby off to bed in their hayloft bedroom. Vic declines—boys mature later than girls. He says he would rather go for a walk, but Wilma reminds him that it's raining outside. She taunts him with the accusation that he is afraid to go to the hayloft with her, so to save his not-yet-established manhood, Vic has to follow her.

This leaves Billie Mae feeling lonely and rejected. She tries to get a response from Wilma and Vic, who are oblivious to her calls. She leaves crying, and the stage remains empty and quiet for several minutes before the curtain falls.

Rainy is merely an exercise in characterization. The plot is trivial and the play presents no controlling theme. It is merely a study in the growing-up process, a topic that interested Inge in a great deal of his work. Whereas it takes until middle age for some of Inge's protagonists to reach emotional maturity, this play is concerned only with the attainment of physical maturity and with the situations its attainment creates. The play reads like Inge writing a parody of Inge. When Wilma and Vic disappear into the hayloft, one is reminded of Cora and Rubin's going upstairs in *Dark*.

The Mall

The Mall is another of Inge's slice-of-life plays. Set in a seaside resort after the season is over, the whole action takes place over a period of about twenty minutes. Inge's directions put great emphasis on the autumnal atmosphere of the play. Banners herald the freaks who were part of a show there during the season. These banners look mockingly upon the scene, as do two live freaks, the two old crones who occupy the stage during the play and who unify its action.

Inge indicated that the play's most significant purpose was to examine various kinds of love. In a brief space, he presents and comments on six different kinds of love. The two old crones, the most pervasive element in the play, signify lost love. They still want love. They are voyeuristic, much as Lola was in *Sheba,* and they observe the passing parade so that they can enjoy vicariously some of the love that passes in front of them.

Two matrons exercising on the beach represent conventional, middle-class, married love. The old crones shock them, as do the lovers in the play. These two conventional women, who comment on the passing of summer (youth) and on the wintertime that lies ahead, have probably led less fulfilled existences than the old crones, who at least have lurid memories of their past loves to warm them in winter. By introducing the two matrons early in this short play, Inge sets up his sharpest contrast, that between them and the two crones. One of the crones mocks the matrons in an amusing speech that probably comes close to revealing the truth of their existences.

The most promising love situation in the play is between a sailor and a young girl. The two have a healthy attraction to each other, but they face the kinds of parental objections that Inge introduced into *Grass* and *Bus Riley.* The two want only to be together, but they cannot be because the girl's parents are suspicious if she stays out late. Inge implies here that the best possible love is the kind that two young people feel for each other but that so many obstacles stand in the way of its fulfillment that the innocence and excitement that are part of it are damaged by the difficulties it encounters.

In the remaining characters, Barney, Dell, Clara, and the middle-aged man, Inge presents three more faces of love. Barney has recently been released from a mental hospital, where he apparently landed because he was unable to deal with the rejection he received from a middle-aged streetwalker, Clara. Still in a precarious state of mental health, Barney returns to the mall where he knows Clara will be soliciting. He wants to live with her, to recapture the love he had once experienced with someone much earlier in his life.

But Clara, who is not the type to settle down, has great antipathy for Barney. For her, love is physical, and she wants all the variety she can get. She is at the mall waiting for a man with whom she has a date, someone she will probably never see again. She counters her own loneliness with frequent, casual affairs.

Barney cannot understand or accept Clara's ways. He grabs her, much as Bo grabs Cherie in *Bus Stop,* and passionately declares his love for her. Clara, quite intractable in the face of this annoyance, kicks Barney in the groin and hits him viciously. Dell, Barney's friend and companion, who serves a function similar to that Virgil serves in *Bus Stop,* is with him in the mall when this happens. He represents the platonic love of a close friend, an outgoing love that is selfless and is motivated by genuine concern and caring. Dell wants Barney to fight back when Clara attacks him, but Barney is in love and a man in love has little fight left in him.

Mall is actually a modern morality play. The crones are like allegorical figures out of the Middle Ages. Inge uses them to reflect all the emotional states the action of the play elicits. They weep at young love, mock conventional married love, and are as curious as three-year-olds about the many loves Clara experiences. Their unfulfilled desires make them lecherous. Ugly as gargoyles, they are grim reminders of what life holds.

An Incident at The Standish Arms

An Incident at the Standish Arms tells about how a respectable society divorcée seduces a hapless taxicab driver one mid-afternoon and of the guilt she feels afterwards. The characters in this five-and-a-half-page, one-act play have no names, heightening the sense of anonymity Inge builds in it. The play essentially involves only two characters, although the divorcée's twelve-year-old daughter appears and is given two brief speeches at the play's conclusion.

The man and woman in the play represent two completely different social milieux. She is well-to-do and has social status; he is commonplace and has no social status. Ironically, however, it is the man who has inherent pride and dignity and the woman who is lacking in self-respect. She needs physical satisfaction from a man. Once she receives it, however, she cannot bear to face him. She is consumed with fear that her daughter will come home and discover her with the taxicab driver or that the management of the elegant Standish Arms will become suspicious of her taking him to her apartment with her. The play opens as the woman comes onstage from the bedroom. She seems on the verge of

screaming and is apparently consumed by guilt and conflict. She seems
cornered and trapped, not by the man, but by her own fear and guilt.
Her animal desires are in constant conflict with her need to feel that
she is a good mother and a respectable woman.

The taxicab driver has made no advances toward her; it is she who
has vamped him. He tries to reassure her by telling her that he has
a wife and three kids and that he certainly doesn't want any trouble.
When he pauses to have a drink, he rehearses for the audience the
particulars of their meeting. Shocked at his accurate recounting of how
they met, the woman asks the man to leave by the service elevator so
that no one will see him.

He is reluctant to leave, but agrees to. He wants to kiss her before
he goes, but she cannot bring herself to allow that. The play reaches
its dramatic climax at this point as the man curses her, calls her a
hypocrite, and, grabbing an expensive Chinese vase from the table,
smashes it to the floor. He tells the woman she has made him feel
cheap, which reminds one of Bo's comments to Cherie in *Bus Stop*.

The man shows his inherent dignity and his displeasure at spending
his life in a role inferior to that of people who have less dignity, who
are less honest than he. The woman tries to explain her actions by
saying that she is divorced and misses her husband sexually. When the
man leaves, she collapses on the sofa and sobs. Her daughter then
comes in from school, and the mother resumes her role as the good
mother and respectable woman.

Ironically, the daughter needs to have her write a note to get her
seat changed in school because she has been forced to sit beside a girl
who uses filthy words and who smells because she does not bathe often
enough. The mother promises to write the note, thus bringing the
depiction of upper middle-class hypocrisy full circle. The social commentary in this sharply focused vignette is biting and verges on bitterness.

The Strains of Triumph

The Strains of Triumph derives its title from Emily Dickinson's "Success
Is Counted Sweetest"; the second word in the title has the double
meaning of both "sounds" and "burdens." The play revolves around
a love triangle that includes two college athletes, Ben and Tom, and
Ann, the girl they both love. The triangle, vaguely reminiscent of the
Turk-Bruce-Marie triangle in *Sheba* and the Hal-Alan-Madge triangle
in *Picnic*, never gains real credibility because the play's focus is distorted.

Inge introduces Professor Benoit, an associate in classics, into the play to provide a somewhat generalized parallel to Ben—note the similarity in the names. Professor Benoit tells Ben that he was once in love but that it terrified him because the object of his love was so beautiful, so tender, and so fine that he trembled at her very proximity. Here again are shades of the Madonna complex that Inge has used in other instances, most notably in *Sheba*. In his longest speech, Professor Benoit articulates his theory that all people are either participants in or observers of life. Ben has always participated in the relays that he and Professor Benoit are now watching from the hillside. Ben is humiliated not to be running, but Professor Benoit assures him that it is possible to enjoy the relays without running in them, a sentiment that offers Ben little comfort—who would wish to turn into a Professor Benoit?

Strains suffers from a lack of dramatic intensity as well as from the lack of focus that occurs when Inge gives primary attention first to Ann and Tom and then switches his attention to Ben and Professor Benoit. No one in the play shows deep feelings. Ann and Tom try to include Ben in their activities. Professor Benoit lives his whole life in the emotional middle ground from which he watches the lives of others, a voyeur by choice rather than, like Lola in *Come Back, Little Sheba*, a voyeur of necessity.

Strains is interesting largely for Inge's depiction of Professor Benoit, who seems totally indifferent to Ben's suffering and talks all through Ben's tearful rendition of his past. Professor Benoit, like Professor Lyman in *Bus Stop*, seems seriously flawed, but Inge's approach to professors is consistently stereotypical.

In *Glory*, when professors from the state university warn the town that the mines are bound to give out, the town disparages the judgment. Howie, the bartender, says that no one listens to professors. Charles Barrett is correct in his judgment that "the fact that [Inge] sacrificed his acting career which he wanted so badly in order to prepare himself to teach is probably of significance in his later attitude toward the teaching profession in his plays."[2]

Strains, like most of Inge's plays, deals with banal people in banal settings and situations. However, Inge's great gift was always his ability to give life to such situations and, through his depth of perception, to involve his audiences with them. *Strains* falls short of Inge's usual standard because it does not dig deeply enough into the situation it depicts.

The Disposal and The Last Pad

The Disposal and The Last Pad are essentially the same play.[3] Pad, which was produced off-Broadway at the 13th Street Theater in December 1970, is a somewhat longer version of The Disposal, which was produced off-Broadway in 1973. Pad has three more characters than The Disposal.

The play is set on Death Row in a midwestern prison. The three condemned murderers being held there are Jess, the protagonist, who killed his pregnant wife for no apparent reason; Luke, found guilty of killing a man during a holdup; and Archie, an effeminate homosexual, condemned for murdering his mother and grandmother. The only woman on stage during the action of the play is Mona, Luke's drab wife, who visits him every week, bringing him brownies and religious platitudes. She is a smothering woman, and the dialogue leads one to believe that Archie's mother and grandmother were similar in their ability to rob men of their identities.

During most of the play's action, the three condemned men are alone on stage, trapped in a crucial situation and trapped with each other. Archie constantly offends the moral sensibilities of the others, particularly Luke, who exhibits the prototypical revulsion that macho men display toward gays. Archie taunts the other two continually, although he occasionally relents in the case of Jess because Jess is to be electrocuted tonight.

When Jess is to order his last meal, he doesn't know what he wants to eat, so Archie, who appreciates gourmet food, orders for him and, of course, ends up eating the meal. Archie's date with the electric chair is eight days away, and he refuses to think about it.

Jess's only wish is that his father, who has promised to come to see him, will arrive, although it now seems unlikely that he will because the eleventh hour is nigh and there has been no word from him other than a postcard two weeks earlier saying that he is setting out. The father does arrive, however, just in time to say goodbye to his son and to tell him that he believes in his innocence.

This is not what Jess wants. He readily acknowledges his guilt. Rather, he wants his father to love him even though he has committed murder, but the father is deaf to Jess's protestations and finally leaves this unhappy setting still proclaiming Jess's innocence. He does not leave, however, until he makes sure that he is getting Jess's few possessions, including sixty dollars he direly needs to pay for his motel room.

Shortly afterwards, Jess is hauled off to meet his fate, screaming as he is dragged away, and enumerating the things he does not want to give up, including corn on the cob, which Mel Gussow, in his review of the play, said was "an exact description of that particular moment."[4] The lights dim momentarily as a surge of power is drawn from the prison's electrical system. A new prisoner is brought into Jess's cell, and Archie begins to make gay propositions to him.

These two plays reflect a theme with which Inge was becoming increasingly concerned, that of a man's being confined against his will in a situation from which there is no escape. This existential theme is consciously a part of this play, which bears general similarities to Jean-Paul Sartre's *No Exit* (1947). Archie, the most intelligent of the three prisoners, alludes to the existential philosopher Sören Kierkegaard in one of his speeches, clearly indicating that Inge had Kierkegaard and existentialism on his mind when he wrote the play.

For all its talk about capital punishment and the justice system, for all its overtones of how environment can lead one into criminal behavior, these plays never really delve seriously or deeply into the social issues they suggest. In them, Inge moves toward absurdist writing, toward the nihilism that existentialism suggests. He seemed at odds, however, with his own feelings and was, therefore, unable to bring the play, in either of its versions, to the point at which it could make any sort of productive statement to audiences.

The Call

The Call is essentially a two-person sketch that takes place in New York City.[5] Joe has come from Billings, Montana, to lead the Billings chapter of his lodge in a parade. He wears his lodge's costume. Joe's sister, Thelma, is fast becoming a famous Broadway actress. Her husband, Terry, welcomes Joe in their elegant twenty-second floor apartment, which Joe has reached by walking up from the lobby, carrying a heavy suitcase with him. He doesn't like elevators and will not risk getting trapped in one.

The play is an absurdist interlude. It has almost no action. Terry expresses his hope that Joe will stay with him and Thelma during his visit to New York, but Joe demurs. He doesn't like heights. He clutches his heavy suitcase where he keeps his private things, his keepsakes. Joe appears to be in the early stages of senile psychosis. He is paranoid and distrustful of everyone. He thinks the teenagers on his flight to

New York were doing unnatural things throughout the whole tourist section of the plane. He blames their actions on LSD.

Joe wears Russian boots but protests that he is not a Communist. He refuses to let Terry make a hotel reservation for him, saying that he will know the right place to stay when he sees it. He, as the youngest child in his family, cared for his mother, who has now been dead for some time. Joe misses her and sometimes forgets she is dead. He almost sent her a telegram when he arrived in New York to say that he had arrived safely.

Joe needs to make a telephone call. He dials it when Terry is offstage and the operator tells him there is no such number. He insists that there is such a number and thinks the operator is in league to keep him from making his connection. He complains to Terry that none of his calls go through nowadays, implying that the telephone company does not want him to get through.

The Call is not of much dramatic consequence except in its relationship to two themes that Inge explores elsewhere. Inge had often been confined to hospitals and sanitoria because of his drinking and his emotional upheavals. Confinement in such places made him claustrophobic. Joe's fear of the elevator, his terror at the thought of being trapped in it, is reflected in Inge's other writing. In *Dark* and in his novel, *My Son Is a Splendid Driver,* Inge alludes to the fetus confined to the womb but eager to get out, eager to escape the confinement. In *Sheba,* Doc projects a terror of the drunk tank at the City Hospital, and it is his fear of the drunk tank that makes him come back to Lola and live out his life with her. These incidents are all akin to Joe's fear of the confinement he might experience in a stalled elevator.

The Call is also concerned with the question of privacy. Just as Mr. Newbold demanded his privacy in *The Tiny Closet* and the renter in *A Murder* went so far as to pay five hundred dollars to have a lock installed on his closet door, so does Joe have almost a psychotic obsession with keeping the contents of his suitcase private. The two incidents are remarkably similar and suggest that Inge had the matter of individual privacy much on his mind when he wrote both of these one-act plays.

Inge undoubtedly modeled some of his characters on people he had observed during his confinements in mental facilities, and *The Call* is an example of this kind of character sketch. One of Inge's unpublished plays, *Venus in Therapy,* is also attributable to experiences he had during his own confinements.

A Murder

A Murder is reminiscent of some of Edward Albee's dramas.[6] The dialogue, which reflects the absurdist tradition, is between an unnamed man and, alternately, his new landlady and the houseman, a jack-of-all-trades who puts a lock on the renter's closet door. Inge's dialogue exceeds credibility, as the dialogue often does in absurdist drama. Much of the dialogue in this play reminds one of the recursive, pointless dialogue in Edward Albee's *The Zoo Story* (1960) or in Samuel Beckett's *Waiting for Godot* (1954).

The man, who gives his occupation as "thinker," looks at a room in a commonplace boardinghouse. The landlady virtually coerces him into taking the room, then demands that he complete a long application form, which she actually fills out for him, writing down answers to such questions as "What is your crime?" and "What was your most unhappy day?"

It turns out that the rent for the room is to be one hundred dollars a day. The man protests that he cannot afford such an absurdly high rent, but the landlady tells him that he will get used to paying it. She resolutely refuses to provide him with the secure lock that he insists on having for his closet door, but finally tells him the houseman will install it at the renter's expense. The houseman is said to be away, and the landlady does not know when he will return.

As soon as the landlady leaves, the houseman appears. He has been there all along, and he tells the renter that he should not believe everything the landlady says. The shock comes when he installs the lock and tells the renter that his bill is five hundred dollars. The renter protests, but he writes a check for the absurd amount after the houseman tells him that if he has to remove the lock he has just installed, the removal will cost two hundred dollars more.

When the renter is left alone, he begins to unpack. He opens a bureau drawer and in it finds a dead baby with a sword beside it. He calls the landlady, who can't explain where the dead baby came from. The renter, after holding the dead child close to him, decides that he must move, as he has apparently done continually throughout his pointless life. The landlady says that she will have to charge him for an extra day because he did not give the required day's notice. He writes her a check for two hundred dollars and leaves. During his departure, the houseman demands and gets a tip.

After a taxi whisks the renter away, the landlady goes into his room. She looks in the bureau drawer and finds nothing in it but a pair of the man's pajamas. The baby incident in this play suggests the myth of George and Martha's baby in Edward Albee's *Who's Afraid of Virginia Woolf?* (1962).

Parts of *Where's Daddy?* had verged on theater of the absurd, and at least one critic thought that the play would have been more successful had Inge made it a clearly absurdist drama.[7] Inge was well aware of the absurdist movement, as he demonstrates in *A Murder*, which projects a life that is irrational, illogical, inchoate, and contradictory. The man in the play, who is not even accorded the identity that a name would bestow upon him, lives a life with no apparent meaning or purpose. The starkness of the stage throughout the play also suggests the absurdist theater.

A Murder is as experimental as anything Inge ever wrote. The play is unrealized dramatically, but it is an important part of the Inge canon because it shows the author trying new techniques as he made a despairing attempt to continue writing despite the hostile reception of his plays from *Loss* onward. At this point, absurdist theater mirrored Inge's own increasingly pessimistic view of life and of human purpose.

The Shorter Plays

The shorter plays reflect various stages of William Inge's development as a playwright and some of them suggest the direction his work might have taken had he returned to writing major dramas after recovering from the disappointment of *A Loss of Roses, Natural Affection,* and *Where's Daddy?*. Some of the shorter plays are mere sketches. Others are more fully realized and show true promise. *Bus Riley's Back in Town* was made into a feature film. *The Boy in the Basement* certainly had the makings of a full-length play, but Inge never turned it into one.

Plays like *The Mall; To Bobolink, for Her Spirit; Memory of Summer; An Incident at the Standish Arms; The Call; The Strains of Triumph;* and *The Tiny Closet* develop interesting characters, and at least some of them develop partially a number of the themes that concerned Inge most, particularly the theme of allowing people to maintain their privacy, as it is reflected significantly in *The Tiny Closet, The Call,* and in Inge's absurdist play, *A Murder.* These plays were not meant to be staged, although an interesting evening of theater could result from an offering of two or three of them, particularly the last three mentioned.

The Last Pad is the only one of the shorter plays discussed here that had a significant production, being given not only off-Broadway but also, under the title *Do Not Go Gentle* at the University of California, Los Angeles in the late 1960s and under the title *The Disposal* in the Greenwich Mews Theater in New York City in 1973. The play was revived in California in 1973, shortly after Inge's death.

Although none of these plays is an artistic triumph, a number of them have the possibility of being worked into something of dramatic consequence. One might hope that at least the best of them might one day be produced for audiences interested in Inge's development as a writer.

Chapter Five
The Novels

Nature, she had discovered, equipped men much more generously than
did Praxiteles.

—From *Good Luck, Miss Wyckoff*

William Inge lived for slightly over seven years after *Where's Daddy?*,
his last Broadway play, was rejected by audiences and critics. During
these seven years he made desperate attempts to do the only thing he
wanted to do with his life—to write. He bore indelible scars from the
harsh criticism his plays after 1959 received. He took this criticism
personally and was, quite understandably, deeply wounded by it, given
the cruel and vengeful spirit that characterized much of it. Inge's earlier
plays were occasionally revived during this period, and some of his new
material, such as *Caesarean Operations* (1973), was produced until his
death in 1973. The sparse criticism of these later productions, however,
offered him little encouragement. Mel Gussow, writing of the off-
Broadway production of *The Last Pad,* asked, "What is a new William
Inge play doing off Off Broadway?" He answers the question, "One
thought that perhaps it was too offbeat or controversial for commercial
production. The truth is that it is simply lesser Inge."[1]

By this time, Inge was financially secure and owned a comfortable
home in Beverly Hills. The little college teaching he undertook was
sporadic at best. He never enjoyed teaching. Writing was his life, and
he sensed that if his writing stopped, his life would end. Because he
seemed to have lost his ability to provide Broadway with plays it could
accept, he turned his talents to another genre, and, in his last five years,
wrote three novels, two of them published. The first, *Good Luck, Miss
Wyckoff (Luck),*[2] is really a novella. Containing some forty thousand
words, it had to be padded to bring it even to that length. Although
the book received some generous reviews, it is unevenly written, at
times badly written. Nevertheless, its protagonist, Evelyn Wyckoff, who
reminds one of Rosemary Sydney in *Picnic,* is a well-realized character.
Her anguish, set against the midwestern backdrop in which Inge places
her, is convincing. No one who reads this novel can deny that Inge

understands small-town life in the Midwest as well as any writer who has thus far attempted to depict it.

My Son Is a Splendid Driver (Driver), published a year after *Luck*, is highly autobiographical and is better written than the earlier novel, although Joe, its protagonist, is less memorable than Evelyn Wyckoff, largely because he shares the spotlight throughout the book with other strong and compelling characters. Certainly these two novels are not the work of a writer who had lost his ability to write. Inge, however, viewed himself as a failure, and because neither of these books was an unqualified success, he harbored the grave personal doubts that caused him to attempt suicide several times and ultimately, on 10 June 1973, to succeed in taking his life.

His final novel, *The Boy From the Circus,* has not been published. A publisher returned the manuscript to Inge the day before his death. Inge never opened the package that contained the manuscript and the publisher's letter of rejection. This chapter discusses the two novels now in print.

Good Luck, Miss Wyckoff

Born, bred, and for the most part educated in the Midwest, Evelyn Wyckoff at age thirty-seven has, for the last decade, taught high school Latin in Freedom, Kansas, a town like Independence, Kansas, where Inge himself was raised. Evelyn has a master's degree and has spent some summers at Columbia University working on a doctorate she seems unlikely to attain. For ten years she has rented a room from Mrs. Heming, whose husband, a salesman, spends most of his time on the road. Beth Hughes, another teacher, also rents a room from Mrs. Heming. Evelyn and Beth are close friends.

Now approaching middle age, Evelyn has never had a home of her own. She joins other teachers every night for dinner in one or another of Freedom's few restaurants. Evelyn is still a virgin and is ashamed of the fact. Her circumscribed existence seems destined to continue at an emotional subsistence level for the rest of her days. Unlike Rosemary Sydney in *Picnic,* Evelyn has no Howard to offer her the hope of marriage.

Evelyn is different from the people around her. She made Phi Beta Kappa in college. She has liberal views and is offended by anti-Semitism, even when it is expressed by her Jewish friend and classmate at Columbia, Rebecca Horowitz, who calls one of their mutual acquaintances a "yid," and points out to Evelyn that whatever his ethnic origins, the person she is referring to is obnoxious. Evelyn thinks that interracial marriage should be sanctioned and views it as the obvious solution to racial problems. She is convinced that people of mixed blood are the most promising people.

Despite her liberal tendencies, which run completely counter to what most people in Freedom believe, Evelyn prefers to teach Latin rather than English because of its snob appeal. She is not only a gifted teacher but also an outspoken supporter of unpopular causes. Evelyn is a valued faculty member, one who has always exemplified reason and stability.

When Evelyn turns thirty-five, however, she begins to have irregular menstrual periods and all sorts of emotional problems. Sometimes she bursts unexpectedly into tears and has to leave her classroom in mid-declension to rush to the teachers' lounge where she can give way to her emotions. When she goes to movies with other teachers, she sometimes begins to weep uncontrollably and has to leave her friends behind and rush home because she cannot control herself. Mrs. Heming and Beth Hughes are well aware that a change is taking place in Evelyn. Mrs. Heming wonders whether she will be able to keep Evelyn as a roomer because her gloom now pervades the house.

Largely because Mrs. Heming and Beth urge her to do so, Evelyn goes to her local physician, Dr. Neal, who was a couple of years ahead of her in college. She has long had a crush on him. She tells him about her recent problems and assures him that the irregularity of her periods cannot be on account of pregnancy because she has not had sexual intercourse for some time. Dr. Neal gives her a gynecological examination and, much to his surprise, finds that his finger is blocked from entering her because her hymen is intact.

He then gives her the name of a psychiatrist in Wichita and suggests to her that she might prevent premature menopause by having a sexual relationship if there is anyone she cares enough about to make this feasible. He also acknowledges that she must be circumspect about such a relationship because the discovery that she was having an affair could cost her her job.

Evelyn, portrayed as always being outside any fulfilling experience, starts going to the Wichita psychiatrist, Dr. Rubin, on a regular basis. She comes close to having an affair with the driver whose bus she regularly takes to Wichita for her psychiatric sessions, but she cannot quite bring herself to do so.

Just when it seems that Evelyn is to live and die a virgin, her life takes a drastic turn. Her high school is across the street from a junior college that has attracted to it a fine black athlete, twenty-year-old Rafe Collins. To justify the money the school district has used to attract athletes to the junior college, the institution has given Rafe and several other football players light work to do cleaning up rooms in the high school at the end of each school day. Rafe is extremely good-looking. He is aloof from most people, including his teammates.

One November afternoon, Evelyn has lingered in her classroom to grade papers. Rafe enters the room to clean it. Soon he makes advances to Evelyn, who is both appalled and intrigued. By March, he has seduced Evelyn, whom Dr. Rubin has recently dismissed as being on the way to overcoming her problems. As this illicit affair progresses, Rafe becomes increasingly demanding. He humiliates Evelyn, forcing her to come to him on all fours and beg him for sex. Suffering all the pangs of conscience that her midwestern background evokes, Evelyn, in the span of three weeks, becomes an emotional wreck.

When she calls Dr. Rubin for help, she learns he is away for a week attending a medical convention. She has nowhere to turn. She fears that if she confesses her situation to Dr. Neal, he will be disgusted. She cannot confide in her Presbyterian minister in this small town because he would not understand.

The fact that Rafe is just a little more than half her age and black are significant complicating factors in this threatening situation. Rafe, always the aggressive male animal, has an anger with the world that makes it necessary for him to control and humiliate Evelyn. She is always the protesting but willing passive party in the relationship, which Rafe makes an increasingly complicated and demeaning one. For the first time in her life Evelyn enjoys sexual fulfillment, but she pays a high price for it.

Despite Rafe's threats to tell his teammates about his affair with Miss Wyckoff, he keeps their relationship to himself. His teammates, who share with him the responsibility of cleaning the school, begin to realize what is going on, however, because Rafe disappears into Miss Wyckoff's room every afternoon and stays there so long that he fails to clean the other rooms he is responsible for. His teammates have to cover for him.

The relationship between Rafe and Miss Wyckoff becomes public knowledge when, one day near the end of March, Rafe's teammates hear piteous cries from Miss Wyckoff's room. They try to enter, but the door is locked. One of the teammates uses his pass key to unlock the door, and inside the room they find Rafe and Miss Wyckoff, both naked. Rafe is astride Miss Wyckoff and is pressing her breasts into the steaming radiator, burning her painfully.

Gossip begins to circulate, and Miss Wyckoff is forced to resign her position and face an uncertain future. She pleads with her principal to protect Rafe so that he can finish his education, and the principal acknowledges that Rafe is in trouble with the Board of Education, but that they will likely dismiss his transgression when he makes his first touchdown in the fall, showing clearly the double standard of morality that women like Evelyn face.

In this novel, Inge is concerned with showing the unrealistically high moral standard communities set for teachers. At one point, Miss Wyckoff says that admitting to being a teacher is tantamount to admitting one is a sexual failure. Quite simply, teachers are not permitted to have their own lives. In their parting interview Mr. Havemeyer, the school principal, tells Evelyn that people in the teaching profession are denied the pastimes and pleasures that most people take for granted. He admits to taking an occasional drink, but adds that he never drinks in public.

Inge introduces into the novel a widow in the town, Fern Hudson, whose husband was killed in the South Pacific during the war. Fern, like Dr. Neal, is one of the country club set, and it is rumored that Dr. Neal has had an affair with her. Fern, who has a reputation for sleeping around, is also said to enjoy the bedfellowship of some of the lowlier men in town. Fern, however, is not a teacher, so what she does is not examined with the close scrutiny that Evelyn's actions provoke.

Although *Luck* is in many ways similar to *Picnic*, it differs from it because Evelyn, unlike Rosemary—but certainly with medical sanction—yields to the disturbingly physical male presence Inge introduces into her classroom. In doing so, she sows the seeds of her own destruction. Hal, on the other hand, is loosed into a setting where several sex-starved women are driven to distraction by his half-naked body as he does yard work nearby.

Rather than allow Rosemary to have an affair with Hal, which she would dearly love to do, Inge, playing up a theme common to his early plays, uses Hal to help Rosemary realize that she must accept the compromise Howard represents. No such compromise is available to Evelyn Wyckoff. She looks ahead to three more decades of the lonely existence of a small-town schoolteacher, an existence that will only grow lonelier in her years to retirement. It is true that Evelyn would never have been assertive enough to initiate her devastating affair with Rafe, but she certainly is not strong enough to prevent its happening. She has already missed her chance with the bus driver, who has now, much to her regret, moved to California. She will never have her way with Dr. Neal, although she would like to. When sex with Rafe becomes a possibility, Evelyn cannot foreclose to herself the opportunity to experience the fulfillment Rafe offers.

Everyone—Dr. Neal, Mr. Havemeyer, Mrs. Heming, Beth Hughes—wishes Evelyn Wyckoff good luck, all with the feeling that she will really need it. The best that Evelyn can hope for now is to find a job as far away from Freedom, Kansas, as possible. Mr. Havemeyer suggests that a liberal principal he knows in New Jersey might hire her in spite of what has happened, but Evelyn does not want to leave the Midwest, whose flat terrain, bigoted people, and flat accents she loves despite herself.

At this point, Evelyn is not even sure her parents will take her in, although when she leaves Freedom, she is prepared to go to Belleville, concoct a story about why she is coming home before the end of the school year, and stay with them. She speculates that perhaps eventually she can go to live with her sister, Irma, a high school teacher in Omaha. She thinks Irma might understand her having an affair with a man, but seriously doubts her sister's ability to understand her having an affair with a twenty-year-old black man.

At one point, Evelyn decides to take her own life. She takes a taxicab to Jenkin's Drug Store to fill a prescription for sleeping pills and is humiliated both by the cab driver, a former student of hers to whom she had given a failing grade in Latin, and by some students who are in the drugstore when she arrives. She gets home with her sleeping pills, but decides that she does not hate herself enough to end her life, so instead she swallows a normal dose to help her sleep through a difficult night. Reading about her decision makes one realize how intimately Inge himself has dealt with the sort of decision Evelyn faces.

Throughout the 1960s, William Inge lived in the shadow of his earlier plays. Some of the same critics who complained that he had strayed too far from his sources had earlier expressed their concern that Inge lacked versatility, that he was a playwright who could write only from a limited range of sources. Now that Inge moved to another genre altogether, the critics seemed determined to destroy him further. One reviewer complained that *Luck* seemed like "an outline for one of his plays" and, while admitting that the main character was well developed, attributed that development to "a playwright's depth,"[3] implying certainly that Inge, although he had tried to don a new mantle, had been unable to.

It is interesting to speculate on the sort of reception *Luck* would have received had it been a first novel by an unknown writer. It is likely that its obvious flaws would have been noted but that the book would have been considered a promising beginning because of its strength of characterization and because of the authenticity the author achieves in developing the small-town background.

From 1959 on, Inge went through life the victim of his own past excellence, never to be judged on any but a narrowly comparative basis. He found himself in a no-win situation: if he wrote plays around the themes and characters he understood best, he would be accused of lacking versatility; if he branched out into another medium, he would be criticized for using that medium rather than drama. Because Inge took all of this criticism seriously and personally, it threatened to paralyze him creatively.

My Son Is A Splendid Driver

Inge's disclaimer notwithstanding, *My Son Is a Splendid Driver* is unabashedly autobiographical.[4] Readers who know Inge's plays have already met most of its characters. Uncle Merlin and Aunt Patsy bear strong resemblances to Lottie and Morris in *Dark*. Aunt Patsy lets out her corset the way Lottie does, and her flesh overflows its confinement in great waves. She likes to eat gizzards, which Lottie also gnaws on. Uncle Merlin, like Morris, is a quiet, subdued man with clean hands and well-kept finger nails. Cora and Rubin have their counterparts in Joe Hansen's parents. Joe, the narrator of this memoir that Inge acknowledges to be part truth and part invention, bears striking resemblances to Inge himself.

Uncle Merlin and Aunt Patsy provide insights into the development of Doc and Lola in *Sheba*. Aunt Patsy is an abominable housekeeper and frequently doesn't wash the dishes until the sink is overflowing with pots and pans. Like Lola, she had a little dog, in this case, Fritz. Aunt Patsy is good-hearted. She is childless, sloppy, and gross. Like Lottie, she pretends to be shocked by the pervasive sexuality of Rudolph Valentino, while at the same time finding herself aroused by the very thought of him.

The women Inge knew in the 1920s and 1930s, the women he depicts with admirable authenticity in this book, were not permitted to enjoy sex. For them Victorian prudery was the rule rather than the exception, as Alfred Kinsey found in his survey of the sexual behavior of American women, in which he estimates that fully one-third of all women born between 1900 and 1920 never experienced an orgasm.

Inge's father and Joe's father, Brian Hansen in *Driver,* were both traveling salesmen because they had little to keep them at home. Like Rubin Flood, they stayed away from their families for long stretches, leaving to their wives the responsibility of raising the children and running the household. These fathers were shadowy figures to their children, whose chief identification was with the mother. For the boy children especially, as for Inge himself, the father was the enemy, the competitor for the mother's affections, lavished unrelentingly upon the sons during the father's absences and withdrawn abruptly upon his return.

Brian Hansen, like Rubin Flood, did not have to travel for a living. He could have taken over his father's store in Garden City and run it. Deploring the confinement of such a life, however, he opted to make his living on the road. At the end of *Dark,* Rubin Flood has agreed to take a job in a local store so that he won't have to travel, but if Inge is trying to convince his audience that this is the end of the Floods' problems, he fails utterly. Travel is in Rubin's blood, and his family is unlikely for long to be an adequate substitute for his peccadillos on the road.

In *Driver,* Brian's infidelities when he is away from home are substantiated. A great crisis occurs in the family when Joe is away at college. The Depression has already put the Hansens under financial pressure. It is uncertain that they can afford to keep their son in college. Just at that time, the father is found to have a venereal disease, presumably syphilis, with which he has infected his wife. The two of them now must go for weekly treatments that will last for a year and that will place upon them great financial and emotional strain.

Joe's mother, who suffers a range of phobias that includes heights, Indians, sex, snakes, speed, spirits, storms, and travel, deals with having a venereal disease as though it is the most shameful thing that could happen to a family. In contracting this disease from her husband, her worst fears have been realized. This episode can only confirm her lifelong feeling that sex is dirty and revolting. She now has the ultimate weapon with which to make the rest of her husband's life miserable.

The mother has always idealized her elder son, Jule, the splendid driver referred to in the title. The oedipal situation Inge builds in *Driver* is almost identical to that in *Dark* except that in *Driver*, Jule is older than Sonny. In fact, Jule is old enough to marry, which he does suddenly and secretly, to sidestep the obstacles his mother would predictably put in the path of his giving himself to another woman. A great deal of *Driver* revolves around the fact that Jule develops virulent blood poisoning from a cut he incurs while shaving. He succumbs within three days, leaving his mother to enshrine his memory and ever to compare Joe to this departed paragon. Joe goes through life trying to avoid situations in which such comparisons can be made.

During the family's vacation trip to Colorado Springs, which takes up about a quarter of the book, Jule begins to sleep with a shotgun beside him. When his mother presses him to find out why he does this, he finally confesses to hearing footsteps on the stairs at night. The mother, amazed, says that she has heard footsteps, too, but has not mentioned them to anyone because she feared she was imagining them. As it turns out, the whole family has heard these footsteps, and Bess Hansen now has the courage to mention them to the landlady, Mrs. Salsbury.

When Bess and her son Joe go to Mrs. Salsbury's bungalow to make their complaint, Mrs. Salsbury takes them to see her aged mother, a former spiritualist, who is not surprised at what they have heard. When Bess refers to the noise-makers as "ghosts," the old woman corrects her and calls them "spirits." She denies doing anything actively to summon them, but she says that spirits are always about.

This episode is telling because, although it was Jule, ironically, who brought the whole matter to a head, Joe has to endure for many years to come a relationship with his mother that is dominated by a spirit. After Jule dies, his presence is constant in the mother's life. The other children, and especially Joe, live always in his shadow.

Joe Hansen's older sister, Treva, has been spoiled from birth. The first grandchild on both sides of the family, she was shamelessly indulged. She is now engaged to Clinton Murray, a well-to-do local youth who is away at college, and she rides to Colorado Springs with Clint and his mother in Clint's Cadillac rather than with her family. Like Marie in *Sheba*, Treva, who is hopelessly flirtatious, dates other men while Clint is away at school and finally falls in love with one of them.

Treva's relationship with Clint also resembles Deanie's relationship with Bud in *Splendor*, where a girl from humble origins is in love with a son of the wealthiest family in town. Inge uses the same situation in *Picnic,* in which Madge plans to marry Alan Seymour, who is finishing college and is of the same social standing as Clinton Murray. Despite her wandering ways, Treva marries Clint and their marriage is successful, largely because it provides Treva with the material possessions she values.

Joe Hansen's other sister, Grace, is younger than Treva. She is as painfully shy as Treva is outgoing. She and Reenie in *Dark* come from the same bolt. Grace, who has had half of one of her front teeth knocked off, has gone through life smiling only faintly so that her broken tooth will not show. She has the same sort of fragile mentality as Laura in Tennessee Williams's *The Glass Menagerie.* By the time dental science has progressed to the point that Grace can have her tooth capped, her personality has been formed. She has developed an image of herself as unattractive, and she will carry that image through life with her.

Just as Reenie Flood suffers almost pathological shyness at the thought of having a blind date, Grace dreads any sort of social activity with boys. Just before Reenie's date arrives, she is so upset that she is upstairs vomiting. Cora does not make the situation any better by her constant suggestions of how Reenie should act. In *Driver,* Grace undergoes her mother's coaching as soon as she has accepted any invitation to a party. Social life becomes a humiliation for the shy Grace.

Inge deals directly with the question of homosexuality in *Driver,* showing more aspects of it than he has in any of his previous work. Treva works in a shop owned by the Odgens. Mrs. Ogden plans a buying trip to France shortly before Treva is to marry Clint. She plans to take Treva with her. They get as far as New York City, then Treva comes home quite mysteriously and unexpectedly. It turns out that Mrs. Ogden has made sexual advances to Treva, who flees from the situation.

Inge also reveals that Mr. Ogden, who has had a reputation for consorting with high school boys, eventually comes to be known in town as a pederast. His wife divorces him, and the court gives her everything. She moves away from Freedom, and Mr. Ogden stays in town, a completely ruined man. Inge is working here with a theme that he touched on in the subplot of *Affection* but never developed fully in any of his work.

A second reference to homosexuality involves Joe himself. Away at college, he has joined a fraternity and has to share a bed with one of his fraternity brothers, Bob Luther. Twice Bob moves on Joe sexually, feigning sleep both times. Joe never permits these advances to proceed very far, although in Inge's retrospective narration of them, one senses that perhaps he regrets not having encouraged them.

Evidence of Inge's terror of confinement appears frequently throughout his work, particularly his later work. This terror is inextricably linked with the confinement of the fetus in the womb. In *Driver,* Joe refers to his mother's being quite old when he was born. She held this last of her children in her womb an extra month because having the fetus inside her permitted her to go on feeling that she was young and fertile. Also, she knew that once she had delivered this baby, menopause would overtake her.

Rubin Flood accuses Cora of coddling their children, especially Sonny, and tells her in graphic detail about a mare his father used to have who never wanted to give up her offspring. The mare kept her colts inside her so tenaciously that the farmhands had to reach into her and dig the colts out. The passage in *Driver* that deals with a similar situation, although it is toned down from the comparable passage in *Dark,* is closely akin to it.

The concern with menopause immediately brings to mind, as well, Inge's treatment of Evelyn Wyckoff's possibility of having a premature menopause if she does not have a sexual relationship. Such matters preoccupied Inge, and the settings of his plays consciously reflect the Victorian influences in the lives of his characters. His dramas are often enacted in Victorian parlors, and all of the hypocrisy of Victorian sexual prudery underlies a great deal of his writing.

Just as some critics thought that *Luck* was more a drama than it was a novel, at least one critic suggested that *Driver,* "with its frequent changes of scene, shifts of character and broad time-span . . . reads . . . like a film script."[5] Actually, the same might be said of the dimensions of most well-actualized novels. The novel can usually treat situations in greater depth than films do, and the depth with which Inge approaches the main elements of his narrative in *Driver* is the major difference between it and a film script.

Driver is a much better realized novel than *Luck.* The chief virtue of the earlier novel is that its narrow focus upon its protagonist, Evelyn Wyckoff, is sharp and direct. Evelyn is a more memorable character for example, than, Rosemary Sydney in *Picnic* because Evelyn does not share top billing with any other major characters. *Driver* is a much richer book than *Luck,* however, because, although it depicts an age that has passed, the portrait of the midwestern family is still close enough to many readers to be palpable. In none of Inge's other work does one have a greater sense of the Midwest, of its monotony, of its narrow morality, and of its arcane complexity, than one finds in *Driver*. The psychological development of the characters, particularly of the Jule-Bess-Joe Hansen and of the Jule-Bess-Brian Hansen triangles, is developed with great care, with admirable subtlety, and with a psychological authenticity that makes it compelling.

One critic, who, when he reviewed *Luck*, suggested that Inge should stick to drama, writes, "This second novel . . . causes me to reevaluate that judgment," and goes on to commend Inge's restrained poetic style and his memorable portraits in the book.[6] It is ironic that this last published work of Inge's lifetime holds the same sort of promise critics recognized in *Sheba*. *Driver* is not flawless. Inge works too hard to tie up all the loose ends in a Dickensian way, but the novel's overall thrust and attention to carefully observed and recorded detail make one wish that William Inge had lived to write more novels. He appeared in this one to be on his way to perfecting and broadening his talents perceptibly.

Chapter Six
The Inge Legacy

William Inge was always concerned with producing commercial successes. He once said, "I can never understand this idea that a writer shouldn't try to make money."[1] Inge was willing to compromise at times to assure commercial success, as he did when he capitulated to Josh Logan's urgings and changed the ending of *Picnic* despite his conviction that his original ending was artistically stronger. The notable lack of commercial success of his plays after *The Dark at the Top of the Stairs* troubled Inge less because of lost revenues than because the commercial failure of the later plays indicated to him that he had lost his touch, that he could no longer write plays that audiences would pay to see.

Other playwrights have experienced similar disappointments, but few have suffered from them more than Inge. Paul Green, who forsook Broadway and Hollywood to write highly successful symphonic dramas that are performed regularly in small towns like Manteo and Boone, North Carolina, and Berea, Kentucky, came to feel in the late thirties that the future of American theater was outside New York City, and his regional dramas, performed in resort areas, have attracted large audiences every year for several decades. Clifford Odets continued to write for Broadway after plays like his early social dramas of the thirties were inappropriate for the times. Although he did some excellent writing in plays like *The Big Knife* (1948) and *The Country Girl* (1950), his later work was always compared unfavorably to his angry social dramas of the depression era. A public that castigates a playwright for not being versatile is just as likely to reject the same playwright's ventures into something new.

Tennessee Williams continued to write after his halcyon period, but his later plays drifted further and further from reality. They bewildered audiences more often than they enlightened them. Arthur Miller never recaptured the success he experienced with *Death of a Salesman* (1949), even though *The Crucible* (1953), *The Misfits,* (1961), and *After the Fall* (1963) were sufficiently successful to keep his reputation alive.

Inge should have been encouraged that his first film scenario, *Splendor in the Grass,* won an Academy Award for scriptwriting. His heart, however, was always in Broadway, despite his later protestations to the contrary. No matter what successes accrued to him outside New York, Inge could never feel legitimately successful. That he never had a Broadway success after he had won his Academy Award vitiated for him the glory of having won that award.

When Inge finally moved to writing novels, he seemed to do so because in this medium, he considered himself to be less at the mercy of directors, actors, designers, and perfidious audiences and critics than he was as a playwright. When his novels failed to gain for him the sort of artistic recognition and audience acceptance that his early plays had, he had nowhere to turn. His life was over because, from his point of view, his writing was over.

Inge's Themes

Inge's plays and his two novels are vitally concerned with their protagonists' alienation from society. The alienation Inge presents has various bases, but the theme is constant in his work. He often writes about a circular alienation, as seen in the problems of such characters as Doc Delaney, who drinks because he is alienated and is alienated because he is a drunk. Similarly, a character like Dr. Lyman pursues young girls to overcome the loneliness his alienation causes, yet it is partly because he pursues young girls that he feels alienated. It is through his circular view of alienation that Inge constructs the traps in which many of his major characters find themselves. The only escape from the trap Inge sets is to settle for life on less-than-ideal terms.

To this extent, Inge's point of view is naturalistic. Social determinism creates the situations within which people must function, and the situations are far from perfect—or even desirable. The extent to which Inge's characters try to change their situations varies from his earliest work to his later writing, and his view grows increasingly pessimistic. It is interesting, in this regard, to compare Rosemary Sydney with Evelyn Wyckoff. Both are in essentially the same situation: they are unmarried schoolteachers in a small midwestern town where everyone knows everyone else's business and where schoolteachers are expected to be paragons of virtue, upholding the codes of middle-class morality. Both are sexually frustrated, but more than that, they are frustrated at not being in charge of their own destinies—they live in rented rooms, they eat their dinners in dank restaurants with other schoolteachers, and they conform to the demands of society.

In Evelyn Wyckoff, however, Inge presents a figure about to burst out of the socially imposed shell in which she finds herself. She is a much more free-thinking woman than Rosemary. She advocates mixed marriages, she deplores anti-Semitism, she broadens her horizons by going off to New York to study in the summer. Ultimately, despite her nagging midwestern moral reservations against it, she has an affair, whereas Rosemary solves her problem by marrying someone she does not love. Evelyn not only has an affair, which in itself would be grounds for her dismissal as a teacher, but she has it with a black man almost twenty years younger than she. And, whereas Rosemary's marriage to Howard will give her some of the things she wants, primarily a house of her own, Evelyn's affair can lead only to disaster.

In his later work, however, Inge seems to realize that the compromises he imposed upon his characters in his earlier work offer no solutions, merely continuance. In Evelyn Wyckoff, Inge presents a sexually frustrated woman who is willing to risk everything for the fulfillment her affair brings her, but in doing so, she loses everything, including, of course, her young lover.

Cora Flood in *Dark at the Top of the Stairs* is able to go off with Rubin for a night of love that Inge suggests will lead to a solution of their long-standing problems; Rosemary in *Picnic* is able to justify marrying a respectable man who will provide her with company and some security, but with little excitement; Lola Delaney in *Come Back, Little Sheba* can justify taking Doc back because they need each other; Cherie in *Bus Stop* is able to abandon her career and go off to Montana with Bo, but only because her career is just about over. Evelyn Wyckoff, however, cannot make the kinds of compromises her counterparts in Inge's earlier plays made. She is going to taste life even if doing so leads to her downfall, and it is in this significant difference that a new direction begins to emerge in Inge's viewpoint. All the characters in his early plays settle for lives of quiet desperation; Evelyn shares their desperation, but she strikes out against it, demands her moment of satisfaction no matter what the consequences.

Inge was keenly, personally aware of alienation, loneliness, and isolation. His writing emphasizes these themes, which are intensified in his work by the inability of his characters to communicate with each other in any really satisfactory way. Other underlying themes recur in the whole of Inge's work, among which the most prominent reflects fear of confinement. Doc Delaney fears the drunk tank more than anything else. Cora Flood confines Sonny emotionally, much like the mare who would not give up her colt or like Joe's mother in *Driver,* who is a month late in delivering her own child because she knows its birth will mark the end of her being functionally a woman. *The Last Pad* focuses on confinement and on social justice, and suggests that one of Inge's greatest and most continuing concerns had to do with people's losing their freedom and being confined, a fear intensified certainly by the confinements that his alcoholism and drug dependency had imposed upon him.

Inge's Characters

Although the ideas in Inge's writing are significant, his chief concern was always with characters. His themes and plots consistently develop from his character sketches, which are the basis for all of his writing, as a number of his undeveloped one-act plays reveal. Inge observed people closely and accurately. His highly autobiographical novel, *My Son Is a Splendid Driver,* indicates that the basic gallery of Inge's characters is quite small and consists largely of members of his own family. However, he was able to manipulate and fictionalize these characters so that he could use them over and over. There exists a close kinship among many of the characters in his writing.

Inge once said he felt a duty to find all he could "in the human lives that I know and are available to me—to find the meanings in those lives secondarily. I'll always have to work that way rather than to take a theme and work in the characters secondarily."[2] In most of Inge's work, theme grows naturally and spontaneously from close characterization.

Authors like T. S. Eliot, Clifford Odets, Elmer Rice, Edward Albee, and Eugene O'Neill used their characters largely as vehicles for the presentation of their ideas, and often their characters were subjugated to the ideas they were wrestling with. Inge, on the other hand, concentrated on creating Rembrandt-like portraits from which the ideas proceeded, much as Tennessee Williams did in his best plays.

Inge's strongest depictions are of female characters, particularly of sexually frustrated ones who have little control over their own destinies. If they controlled and sometimes emasculated their men, as Robert Brustein contended,[3] they did so because their men needed taming. Janet Juhnke's objections to this portrayal on feminist grounds,[4] while well argued, lose sight of the fact that many raucous men settle down when they attach themselves to one woman, and this observable fact of life was not lost on Inge.

Inge never married, and perhaps he was overly sensitive to the domination of women because he had a controlling mother who, on account of his father's regular absences, exercised an autocratic authority over her family. Inge, however, often looked to strong women, like Audrey Wood or Margo Jones, for artistic advice and guidance. His unresolved attitude toward his homoerotic tendencies seems also to have played a part in his attitude toward women.

Certainly one cannot read much of Inge without realizing that the battle of the sexes is prominent in his work and that women are usually the victors, although Evelyn Wyckoff, and, to some extent, Sue Barker deviate from this pattern. Most of Inge's women are bent on showing their independence—Rosemary Sydney, Sue Barker, Helen Baird—or they are bent on dominating their men because of the structures of their own egos—Lola Delaney, Lottie Lacey, Cora Flood, Mrs. Loomis, Mrs. Scranton, and Sue Barker, who comes closer to being a modern woman than any other of Inge's female characters.

Inge's first major male character, Doc Delaney, was much overshadowed by his wife. Lola was the undeniable center of *Sheba* and, despite the large number of lines given to him and despite the intense drama of his drunk scene, Doc could not compete with Lola for center stage. In his next play, Inge created in Hal a figure of much less dramatic stature than Doc, and the other men, Howard and Alan, surely offer no competition to the women in *Picnic*.

In *Bus Stop*, the spotlight is on Cherie, although two of the secondary male characters, Professor Lyman and Virgil Blessing, have interesting roles and contribute substantially to the action of the play. Professor Lyman's portrayal is flawed because of the stereotype that Inge had of college professors. This stereotype prevented him from creating rounded characters in his professor types, as one sees in his presentation of Professor Benoit in *The Strains of Triumph*.

In *Dark*, the central male character is Sonny Flood, and even he is quashed by the dominating female when Cora tells him that he can no longer come into her bed at night. Certainly the other two prominent male characters in the play, Rubin and Morris, are overwhelmed by their mates. Sammy remains an undeveloped character because he is seen just long enough for the audience to form of him the superficial opinion that Inge needs to convey if Sammy's suicide is to seem credible.

In Kenny Baird, Inge presents Sonny Flood grown up. Kenny tries to dominate his mother who, like Cora, deals inconsistently with him. Sonny was young enough to have tantrums; Kenny did the next best thing and had an affair with Lila, which represented both his rebellion against his mother and, if we are to believe Inge, his salvation. Donny Barker in *Affection* is cut from the same cloth as Sonny and Kenny, and his rebellion—the senseless murder of a woman—is the most violent and the least successful dramatically.

In both *Loss* and *Affection,* Inge dealt with the oedipal problem that surfaced full blown in *Driver.* However, it is interesting to see how he uses the same situation in *Luck,* where the reader experiences the oedipal situation from the standpoint of the older woman rather from the standpoint of the man, as in the two earlier works.

Inge was most successful in portraying people of the lower middle class, and he is most convincing when he puts them in the Midwest of the twenties. His few excursions away from this class, this time, and this place have lacked the authenticity that helped Inge to create his reputation as an accurate recorder of midwestern life in America, a consummate realist.

Posthumous Productions

Shortly after Inge's death, the Contempo Theater in Los Angeles produced *The Last Pad* and the MET Theater mounted a revival of three of his other plays. Rick Talcove, writing in *The Best Plays of 1973–74,* recalls, "The late William Inge figured prominently during the [1973–74] season with the Contempo Theater's production of *The Last Pad* and the MET Theater . . . discovering theatrical gold by offering three definitive revivals of Inge plays: *The Dark at the Top of the Stairs, Picnic,* and *Bus Stop;* the latter production taking no less than five Los Angeles Drama Critics Circle Awards—a belated tribute to a fine playwright, but a tribute nonetheless."[5]

Since then, Inge's plays have not been revived with such regularity as those of Tennessee Williams or Arthur Miller. Not a year has passed since Inge's death, however, in which the annual volume *The Best Plays of . . .* has failed to list at least one or two revivals of his work. Although *Come Back, Little Sheba, Picnic,* and *Bus Stop* are by far the plays most frequently revived, some of Inge's unpublished shorter plays such as *Caesarean Operations, Central Park,* and *Overnight,* have been included on the programs of experimental theater groups on both coasts. *The Last Pad* was presented off-Broadway in 1987.

During the year of the Bicentennial celebration, 1975–1976, Inge's *Bus Stop* and *Summer Brave* were performed by the American Bicentennial Theater in Washington, D.C., and *Summer Brave* was brought to Broadway between 26 October and 9 November 1975 for a run of sixteen performances at the ANTA Theater.

Over and above the performances recorded in *Best Plays,* Inge is frequently performed by theater groups on college and university campuses. *Picnic* has become a standard offering in summer stock throughout the country, particularly the Midwest. Seldom does a month pass that a film version of at least one Inge play is not offered on cable television. Even *The Stripper,* based on Inge's shunned play, *A Loss of Roses,* is frequent television fare, although *Come Back, Little Sheba* and *Bus Stop* are the two plays most frequently available to television audiences. *Splendor in the Grass,* made from Inge's Oscar-winning film script, is another standard television rerun.

To date, no television specials have been made of any Inge plays, although several would lend themselves well to such treatment, particularly *Come Back, Little Sheba,* a play that has the sort of universality that Miller's *Death of a Salesman* or Williams's *Glass Menagerie* have. Plans were afoot to air *Natural Affection* as a television play, but the script, written in 1971 by Bernard Bassey and authorized by Inge, was never produced, although a successful four-hour television play on a similar theme, based on Pete Hamill's novel, *Flesh and Blood* (1977), was written by Eric Bercovici and aired successfully on national television in 1979, suggesting that the overt presentation of the Oedipus theme is not an insurmountable problem.

A number of Inge's one-act plays, particularly *The Boy in the Basement, The Tiny Closet, Memory of Summer, The Call,* and *The Murder,* would lend themselves to production by college and university groups. The first of these is a most touching and revealing play, and the last two reveal Inge's attempts to work in the absurdist tradition and are of considerable historical significance to those interested in the development of Inge's creative talent.

Notes and References

Chapter One

1. Robert Brustein, "The Men-Taming Women of William Inge," *Harper's,* November 1958, 52.

2. Ibid.

3. Milton Bracker, *New York Times,* 22 March 1953, sec. 2, 1. See also Inge's interview with Digby Diehl in Joseph F. McCrindle, ed., *Behind the Scenes: Theatre and Film Interviews from the Transatlantic Review* (New York: Holt, Rinehart & Winston, 1971), 108–15.

4. Jean Gould, *Modern American Playwrights* (New York: Dodd, Mead & Co., 1966), 265.

5. "Mr. Inge Looks Back," *New York Times Magazine,* 24 November 1957, 80.

6. Bracker, *New York Times,* 22 March 1953, 3.

7. Marilyn Mitchell, "William Inge," *American Imago* 35 (1978):297.

8. Gould, *Playwrights,* 265.

9. Ibid., 265–66.

10. See the foreword to *Four Plays by William Inge* (New York: Random House, 1958), v–vi.

11. "Talk of the Town," *New Yorker,* 4 April 1953, 25–26.

12. McCrindle, *Behind the Scenes,* 110.

13. Charles E. Burgess, "An American Experience: William Inge in St. Louis 1943–1949," *Papers on Language and Literature* 12 (1976):443.

14. These reviews are listed by title in Arthur F. McClure's *William Inge: A Bibliography* (New York: Garland Publishing Co., 1982), 14–37.

15. Tennessee Williams as quoted by Francis Donahue in *The Dramatic World of Tennessee Williams* (New York: Frederick Ungar, 1964), 19. See also Tennessee Williams, *Memoirs* (Garden City, N.Y.: Doubleday & Co., 1975), 89. Williams recalls the date of the meeting as being December 1944. However, Inge's first article on Williams, "St. Louis Personalities: 'Tennessee' Williams, Playwright, Author," *St. Louis Star-Times,* 11 November 1944, 11, was presumably based on this first interview, which took place at Williams's parents' home and was followed by Williams's visit to Inge's St. Louis apartment. The first meeting between the two must have been a month earlier than Williams recollects.

16. Tennessee Williams, "The Writing Is Honest," introduction to *The Dark at the Top of the Stairs* (New York: Random House, 1958), vii–ix. In a letter to Donald Windham dated 15 March 1945, Williams writes, "I went out every night during my week at home [in St. Louis] with Inge and

an amazing widow. . . . ." See *Tennessee Williams's Letters to Donald Windham, 1940–1965* (New York: Holt, Rinehart, & Winston, 1977), 167.

17. Donald Spoto, *The Kindness of Strangers: The Life of Tennessee Williams* (Boston: Little, Brown & Co., 1985), 225.

18. Spoto, *Kindness,* 305–6. See also Williams's comments about Inge as found in "Tennessee Williams' Tribute to Playwright William Inge, Who Died on June 10," *New York Times,* 1 July 1973, sec. 2, p. 3.

19. Williams, "The Writing Is Honest," ix.

20. Audrey Wood with Max Wilk, *Represented by Audrey Wood* (Garden City, N.Y.: Doubleday & Co., 1981), 222.

21. Williams, "The Writing Is Honest," ix. See also Williams's *Memoirs,* 689, and Donahue's *Dramatic World,* 20.

22. Spoto, *Kindness,* 112.

23. Bracker, *New York Times,* 22 March 1953, 3.

24. McCrindle, *Behind the Scenes,* 110.

25. Ibid.

26. Mitchell, "William Inge," 297.

27. Williams, *Memoirs,* 89.

28. Phyllis Anderson, "Diary of a Production," *Theatre Arts* 34 (November 1950):58.

29. Williams, *Memoirs,* 89.

30. *Four Plays,* vi.

31. "Concerning Labels," *New York Times,* 23 July 1950, sec. 2, p. 1.

32. Myles Standish reviewed the play negatively in the *St. Louis Post-Dispatch,* 11 February 1948.

33. "*Picnic:* From 'Front Porch' to Broadway," *Theatre Arts* 38 (April 1954):33.

34. " 'Picnic': Of Women," *New York Times,* 15 February 1953, sec. 2, p. 3.

35. *Four Plays,* ix.

36. Ibid., x.

37. *Time,* 14 March 1955, 58.

38. See Inge's comments on this matter in *Four Plays,* viii. Note also Henry Hewes's statement in "Mr. Inge's Meringueless Pie," *Saturday Review,* 19 March 1955, 24.

39. Spoto, *Kindness,* 225.

40. Naomi Barko, "William Inge Talks about *Picnic,*" *Theatre Arts* 37 (July 1955):67.

41. *Four Plays,* vii–ix.

42. "Defector," *Newsweek,* 14 May 1962, 110.

43. Ibid.

44. "More on the Playwright's Mission," *Theatre Arts* 42 (August 1958):19.

45. "Candidates for Prizes: 9 Younger Playwrights," *Vogue*, 1 May 1954, 135.

46. "*Picnic:* From 'Front Porch' to Broadway," 33.

47. "How Do You Like Your Chopin?" *New York Times*, 27 February 1955, sec. 2, p. 3.

48. McCrindle, *Behind the Scenes*, 111–12.

49. *Los Angeles Times*, 11 June 1973, 17. See Marilyn Mitchell, "The Teacher as Outsider in the Works of William Inge," *Midwest Quarterly* 17 (1976):392, for a brief account by his colleague Robert Cohen of Inge's teaching at the University of California, Irvine.

50. *Library Journal*, 1 May 1971, 1760.

51. Letter from William Inge to me, New York City, 6 October 1963.

52. Lloyd Steele, "William Inge: The Last Interview," *Los Angeles Free Press*, 22 June 1973, 18–22.

53. Letter from Helene Connell to me, Los Angeles, California, 10 June 1974. Connell's italics.

54. Spoto, *Kindness*, 225.

Chapter Two

1. Harold Clurman, *Lies Like Truth* (New York: Macmillan Co., 1958), 14.

2. Donahue, *Dramatic World*, 20.

3. Foreword to *Four Plays*, v.

4. McCrindle, *Behind the Scenes*, 115.

5. "More off the Playwright's Mission," *Theatre Arts* 42 (August 1958):19.

6. Willard Thorpe, *American Writing in the Twentieth Century* (Cambridge: Harvard University Press, 1960), 102.

7. "Talk of the Town," *New Yorker*, 4 April 1953, 24.

8. See, for example, John Gassner, *Theatre at the Crossroads* (New York: Holt, Rinehart & Winston, 1960), 307, and Gerald Weales, *American Drama Since World War II* (New York: Harcourt, Brace & World, 1962), 46.

9. McCrindle, *Behind the Scenes*, 113.

10. "The Schizophrenic Wonder," *Theatre Arts* 34 (May 1950):23.

11. As quoted by Richard Maney in "Blackmer's Scene," *New York Times*, 2 April 1950, sec. 2, 3.

12. *Come Back, Little Sheba* (New York: Random House, 1950), 15; page references are hereafter cited parenthetically in the text.

13. "Schizophrenic Wonder," 23.

14. Some representative contemporary assessments of the play are as follows: Phyllis Anderson, "Diary of a Production," *Theatre Arts* 34 (November 1950):58–59; Brooks Atkinson, "Two Actors," *New York Times*, 26 February

1950, sec. 2, p. 1; William H. Beyer, "The State of the Theatre: Dance, Stage, and the 'Drama-goes-Round,' " *School and Society* 71 (3 June 1950):342–46; Harold Clurman, "A Good Play," *New Republic,* 13 March 1950, 22–23; Wolcott Gibbs, "The Dream and the Dog," *New Yorker,* 25 February 1950, 68, 70; "New Play," *Newsweek,* 27 February 1950, 74; "New Play in Manhattan," *Time,* 27 February 1950, 81; and Kappo Phelan, "The Stage," *Commonweal,* 3 March 1950, 558.

15. McCrindle, *Behind the Scenes,* 110.

16. *Picnic* and *Summer Brave* are treated together because they are different versions of the same play. Page references to *Picnic* (cited in parentheses as *P* followed by page number) are to the version in *Four Plays by William Inge.* Page references to *Summer Brave* (cited parenthetically as *SB* followed by page number) are to *Summer Brave and Eleven Short Plays* (New York: Random House, 1962).

17. See Ralph F. Voss, "William Inge and the Savior/Specter of Celebrity," *Kansas Quarterly* 18 (Fall 1986):27.

18. As quoted in W. David Sievers, *Freud on Broadway* (New York: Hermitage House, 1955), 354.

19. Naomi Barko, "William Inge Talks About *Picnic,*" *Theatre Arts* 37 (July 1953):63.

20. Audrey Wood with Max Wilk, *Represented by Audrey Wood,* 227.

21. Jerry L. Crawford, "An Analysis of the Dramatic Structure of Three Plays by William Inge," unpublished M.A. thesis in speech and drama, Stanford University, 1957.

22. For an insightful consideration of Hal Carter, see Philip M. Armato, "The Bum as Scapegoat in William Inge's *Picnic,*" *Western American Literature* 10 (Winter 1976):273–82.

23. For an explication of this theme in the play, see Barko, "William Inge," 67.

24. See, for example, Janet Juhnke's quite angry article, "Inge's Women: Robert Brustein and the Feminine Mystique," *Kansas Quarterly* 18 (Fall 1986):103–12.

25. Among the most representative comments on *Picnic* are the following: Brooks Atkinson, "Inge's *Picnic,*" *New York Times,* 1 March 1953, sec. 2, p. 1; Eric Bentley's review in *New Republic,* 16 March 1953, 23; Harold Clurman, "Theatre," *Nation,* 7 March 1963, 212–13; Wolcott Gibbs, "Something Old, Something New," *New Yorker,* 28 February 1953, 65–66; Richard Hayes, "The Stage," *Commonweal,* 20 March 1953, 603; Walter Kerr's review in *New York Theatre Critics' Reviews, 1953,* 350; Theophilus Lewis, "Theatre," *America,* 7 March 1953, 622–33; Theophilus Lewis, "Theatre," *America,* 2 May1953, 147; George J. Nathan, "Director's Picnic," *Theatre Arts* 37 (May 1953):14–15; "New Play in Manhattan," *Time,* 2 March 1953, 72, 74; "*Picnic:* More Fun," *Saturday Review,* 7 March 1953,

33–34; *"Picnic* Tells Conquest of a Kansas Casanova," *Life,* 16 March 1953, 136–37; "Reviews," *Newsweek,* 2 March 1953, 84. Walter Kerr's review is also reproduced in Barnard Hewitt's *Theatre U. S. A., 1668–1957* (New York: McGraw-Hill, 1959), 459–61.

26. All references to *People in the Wind* (cited in parentheses as *PW* followed by page number) are to the version that appears in *Summer Brave and Eleven Short Plays;* references to *Bus Stop* (cited in parentheses as *B* followed by page number) are to the first edition of the play (New York: Random House, 1955).

27. McCrindle, *Behind the Scenes,* 114.

28. *Four Plays,* viii; McCrindle, *Behind the Scenes,* 114.

29. Gassner, *Theatre at the Crossroads,* 308.

30. Gerald Weales discusses the symbolism of the names in *Bus Stop* in *American Drama,* 48ff.

31. Theophilus Lewis, *America,* 9 April 1955, 54.

32. Eric Bentley, *New Republic,* 2 May 1955, 22.

33. Richard Watts, *New Theatre Critics' Review, 1955,* 347.

34. Weales, *American Drama,* 44.

35. Gassner, *Theatre at the Crossroads,* 307.

36. Brustein, "The Men-Taming Women," 55.

37. "New Play in Manhattan," *Time,* 14 March 1955, 58.

38. Hewes, "Mr. Inge's Meringueless Pie," 24.

39. McCrindle, *Behind the Scenes,* 114.

40. Brooks Atkinson, "Mr. Inge in Top Form," *New York Times,* 13 March 1955, 58.

41. Among the most significant reviews of the play during its initial Broadway run are the following: "Best Comedy of the Season," *Life,* 28 March 1955, 77–80; Wolcott Gibbs, "Inge, Ibsen, and Some Bright Children," *New Yorker,* 12 March 1955, 62, 64, 66–68; Robert Hatch, "Theatre," *Nation,* 19 March 1955, 245–46; Richard Hayes, "The Stage," *Commonweal,* 8 April 1955, 14; "Love at the 'Bus Stop,' " *New York Times Magazine,* 20 March 1955, 59; "On Broadway," *Newsweek,* 12 March 1955, 99; and Maurice Zolotow, "The Season On and Off Broadway," *Theatre Arts* 39 (May 1955):21–22, 87–88.

42. Gassner, *Theatre at the Crossroads,* 171.

43. *Four Plays,* ix.

44. Ibid.

45. *The Dark at the Top of the Stairs* (New York: Random House, 1958), 53; page references are hereafter cited parenthetically in the text.

46. Winifred Dusenbury, *The Theme of Loneliness in Modern American Drama* (Gainesville: University of Florida Press, 1960), 16–26.

47. Gassner, *Theatre at the Crossroads,* 171.

48. Ibid., 172.

49. Richard Hayes, "A Question of Reality," *Commonweal*, 14 March 1958, 616. Additional contemporary commentary on the play can be found in the following: Harold Clurman, "Theatre," *Nation*, 21 December 1957, 483–84; "The Dark at the Top of the Stairs," *Theatre Arts* 42 (February 1958):20–21; Patrick Dennis, "A Literate Soap Opera," *New Republic*, 30 December 1957, 21; Tom F. Driver, "Hearts and Heads," *Christian Century*, 1 January 1958, 17–18; Wolcott Gibbs, "The Crowded Stairway," *New Yorker*, 14 December 1957, 83–85; Henry Hewes, "Light in the Living Room," *Saturday Review*, 21 December 1957, 27; "New Play in Manhattan," *Time*, 12 December 1957, 42, 44; "The World of William Inge," *Theatre Arts* 42 (July 1958):62–64.

50. Brustein, "The Men-Taming Women," 56.

Chapter Three

1. *Four Plays*, vi.

2. Marilyn Mitchell, "The Teacher as Outsider in the Works of William Inge," *Midwest Quarterly* 17 (1976):392.

3. Juhnke's reaction to Brustein's 1958 article is found in "Inge's Women: Robert Brustein and the Feminine Mystique," *Kansas Quarterly* 18 (Fall 1986):103–11.

4. William Gibson, "For Bill Inge," *New York Times*, 24 July 1973, 35, as cited in Voss, "William Inge and the Savior/Specter of Celebrity," *Kansas Quarterly* 18 (Fall 1986):36.

5. Letter from Helene Inge Connell to me, Los Angeles, Calif., 10 June 1974.

6. Inge to me, [Los Angeles], 20 May 1965.

7. *A Loss of Roses* (New York: Bantam, 1963), 22; page references are hereafter cited parenthetically in the text. The original edition of *Loss* was published by Random House in 1963.

8. Weales, *American Drama*, 45.

9. Ibid.

10. Tom Driver details some of these in "Wanted: Fresh Air," *Christian Century*, 2 January 1960, 15–16.

11. Jean Gould writes in *Playwrights*, "One cannot help wondering why William Inge could not have written a truly dramatic play based on Lila's background and experiences with the tent show. . . . A good play still has to be written about tent-show life, or about a resident stock company in the middle-sized Midwestern town; and Inge seems admirably suited to the task" (272).

12. *Splendor in the Grass* (New York: Bantam, 1961), 8; page references are hereafter cited parenthetically in the text.

13. Harold Clurman, "Theatre," *Nation*, 2 December 1957, 483.

14. *Natural Affection* (New York: Random House, 1963), ix; page references are hereafter cited parenthetically in the text.

15. Edith Isaacs, "Going Left with Fortune," *Theatre Arts Monthly* 19 (May 1935):328.

16. Howard Taubman, "The Theatre: *Natural Affection*," *New York Times*, 2 February 1963, 5.

17. As quoted in *New York Theatre Critics' Reviews* 24 (4 March 1963):383.

18. Ibid., 384.

19. Letter from Inge to me, [Los Angeles], 20 May 1965.

20. Lloyd Steele, "William Inge: The Last Interview," *Los Angeles Free Press*, 22 June 1973, 22.

21. Ibid.

22. *Where Daddy?* (New York: Random House, 1966), 3; page references are hereafter cited parenthetically in the text.

23. As quoted in Burgess, "William Inge in St. Louis," 462.

24. As quoted in Mitchell, "The Teacher as Outsider in . . . Inge," 392.

25. Burgess, "William Inge in St. Louis," 456.

26. "A Question of Identity," *New Republic*, 26 March 1966, 36.

27. As quoted in Burgess, "William Inge in St. Louis," 456.

28. Morris Freedman, *American Drama in Social Context* (Carbondale: Southern Illinois University Press, 1971), 86.

29. Henry Hewes, "Daddyhood," *Saturday Review*, 19 March 1966, 55.

30. Walter Kerr, *The Theatre in Spite of Itself* (New York: Simon & Schuster, 1963), 238–40, passim.

31. "Natural Affection," *Theatre Arts* 47 (March 1963):59.

32. John McCarten, "Tour de Force," *New Yorker*, 9 February 1963, 66.

Chapter Four

1. *Summer Brave and Eleven Short Plays*, x; further page references to all the short plays except *Glory in the Flower*, *The Disposal*, and *The Last Pad* are to this volume. References to *Glory in the Flower* are to the version printed in *24 Favorite One-Act Plays*, ed. Bennett Cerf and Van H. Cartmell (New York: Doubleday & Co., 1958). References to *The Disposal* are to the version printed in *Best Short Plays of the World Theatre, 1958–1967*, ed. Stanley Richards (New York: Crown Publishers, 1968). *The Last Pad*, which is a version of *The Disposal*, has not been published.

2. Charles M. Barrett, "William Inge, The Mid-Century Playwright," unpublished master's thesis in drama, University of North Carolina at Chapel Hill, 1957, 25.

3. Another version of the play was entitled *Do Not Go Gentle.*

4. Mel Gussow, "Theater: 'The Last Pad,' " *New York Times,* 8 December 1970, 61.

5. *The Call* is included in William Inge, *Two Short Plays* (New York: Dramatists' Play Service, 1968), 5–19.

6. Ibid., 23–45.

7. Hewes, "Daddyhood," 55.

Chapter Five

1. Gussow, "Theater: 'The Last Pad,' " 61.

2. *Good Luck, Miss Wyckoff* (Boston: Little, Brown & Co., 1970).

3. Haskel Frankel, "A Playwright's Novel—No, Novella," *New York Times,* 14 June 1970, 24.

4. *My Son Is a Splendid Driver* (Boston: Little, Brown & Co., 1971).

5. Mitchell, "William Inge," 297.

6. Robert Clayton, *Library Journal,* 1 May 1971, 1636.

Chapter Six

1. "Defector," *Newsweek* 14 May 1962, 110.

2. *New York Times,* 22 March 1953, sec. 2, p. 3.

3. Brustein, "The Men-Taming Women, 52–57.

4. Juhnke, "Inge's Women: Robert Brustein and the Feminine Mystique," 103–11.

5. Rick Talcove, *The Best Plays of 1973–74* (New York: Dodd, Mead and Company, 1974).

Selected Bibliography

Because a full, detailed bibliography of William Inge's writing and of writing about him is easily available in Arthur F. McClure's *William Inge: A Bibliography* (New York: Garland Publishing Co., 1982), this bibliography makes no attempt to be comprehensive. McClure covers most of the cogent materials in print about Inge to 1981 and leads the reader to the sources in which all of Inge's published plays are available. He provides a useful list of Inge's 417 reviews published in the *St. Louis Star-Times* during Inge's employment by that paper from 15 June 1943 until 9 February 1946. The bibliography below updates McClure's by citing articles and portions of books that consider Inge from 1981 to 1986, as well as the most salient items from this indispensable book.

PRIMARY SOURCES

Collected Works

Four Plays by William Inge. New York: Random House, 1958; London: William Heinemann, 1960. This volume contains Inge's foreword, as well as printed versions of his first four Broadway productions: *Come Back, Little Sheba: Picnic; Bus Stop;* and *The Dark at the Top of the Stairs*.

Plays

Bus Stop. New York: Random House, 1955; Bantam, 1956. Reprinted in *Theatre Arts* 40 (October 1956):33–56.
The Call. In *Two Short Plays: The Call, and A Murder*. New York: Dramatists' Play Service, 1968.
Come Back, Little Sheba. New York: Random House, 1950. Reprinted in *Theatre Arts* 34 (November 1950):60–88.
The Dark at the Top of the Stairs. New York: Random House, 1958; Bantam, 1958. Reprinted in *Theatre Arts* 43 (September 1959):34–60.
The Disposal. In *The Best Short Plays of the World Theatre, 1958–1967*, edited by Stanley Richards. New York: Crown Publishers, 1968.

Farther Off From Heaven. Unpublished play, 1947.

Glory in the Flower. In *24 Favorite One-Act Plays,* edited by Bennett Cerf and Van H. Carmell. New York: Doubleday & Co., 1958.

A Loss of Roses. New York: Random House, 1960; Bantam, 1963. Reprinted in *Esquire,* January 1960, 138–44.

The Mall. Esquire January 1959, 75–78. See also *Summer Brave and Eleven Short Plays,* below.

Midwestern Manic. In *Best Short Plays, 1969,* edited by Stanley Richards. Philadelphia: Chilton, 1969.

A Murder. In *Two Short Plays: The Call, and A Murder.* New York: Dramatists' Play Service, 1968.

Natural Affection. New York: Random House, 1963.

Picnic. New York: Random House, 1953; Bantam, 1956.

Splendor in the Grass [screenplay]. New York: Bantam, 1961.

Summer Brave and Eleven Short Plays. New York: Random House, 1962. This volume contains these plays in the order given: *Summer Brave; To Bobolink, For Her Spirit; People in the Wind; A Social Event; The Boy in the Basement; The Tiny Closet; Memory of Summer; Bus Riley's Back in Town; The Rainy Afternoon; The Mall; An Incident at the Standish Arms;* and *The Strains of Triumph.*

To Bobolink, For Her Spirit. Included in *New Directions in Prose and Poetry,* 12 (1950). New York: New Directions. See also *Summer Brave and Eleven Short Plays,* above.

Where's Daddy? New York: Random House, 1966.

Novels

Good Luck, Miss Wyckoff. Boston and Toronto: Little, Brown & Co., 1970; London: Deutsch, 1971; New York: Bantam, 1971.

My Son Is a Splendid Driver. Boston and Toronto: Little Brown & Co., 1971.

Selected Articles

"The American Scene." *Glamour,* May 1962, 111.

"Concerning Labels." *New York Times* 23 July 1950, sec. 2, p. 1.

"How Do You Like Your Chopin?" *New York Times,* 27 February 1955, sec. 2, p. 3.

"More on the Playwright's Mission." *Theatre Arts* 42 (August 1958):19.

"Most Promising Playwright." *New York Times,* 23 July 1950, sec. 2, p. 1.

"*Picnic:* From 'Front Porch' to Broadway." *Theatre Arts* 38 (April 1954):32–33.

" 'Picnic': Of Women." *New York Times,* 15 February 1953, sec. 2, p. 3.

"The Playwright, His Mission." United States Information Service, 1956.

"The Schizophrenic Wonder." *Theatre Arts* 34 (May 1950):22–23.

Manuscript Sources

"David Belasco and the Age of Photographic Realism in the American Theatre." Unpublished Master's thesis in English. George Peabody College for Teachers, Nashville, Tennessee, 1936.
The chief manuscript collections of Inge's work and of work relating to him are housed in the William Inge Collection, Independence Community College, Independence, Kansas; in the Kansas Collection in the Spencer Research Library, University of Kansas, Lawrence; and in the Humanities Research Center, University of Texas, Austin.

SECONDARY SOURCES

Books and Parts of Books

Broussard, Louis. *American Drama: Contemporary Allegory from Eugene O'Neill to Tennessee Williams.* Norman: University of Oklahoma Press, 1962. Contends that Inge's greatest literary kinship is with T. S. Eliot in his interest in the commonplace.
Clurman, Harold. *Lies Like Truth.* New York: Macmillan, 1958. Clurman, who directed *Bus Stop,* is chiefly concerned with *Picnic* here, and considers it a solid success.
Dusenbury, Winifred L. *The Theme of Loneliness in Modern American Drama.* Gainesville: University of Florida Press, 1960. Perceptive writing about Lola's loneliness in *Sheba.*
Diehl, Digby. "Interview with William Inge." In Joseph McCrindle, *Behind the Scenes: Theatre and Film Interview from Transatlantic Review.* New York: Holt, Rinehart & Winston, 1971, 108–15.
Donahue, Francis. *The Dramatic World of Tennessee Williams.* New York: Frederick Ungar Publishing Co., 1964. Frequent references to Inge and to Williams's friendship with him.
Fernandez, James W. "The Dark at the Bottom of the Stairs: The Inchoate in Symbolic Inquiry and Some Strategies." In Jacques Maquet, ed., *On Symbols in Anthropology: Essays in Honor of Harry Hoijer, 1980.* Malibu, Calif.: Undena, 1982, 13–43. Gives full attention to the symbolism in *The Dark at the Top of the Stairs.*
Freedman, Morris. *American Drama in Social Context.* Carbondale: Southern Illinois University Press, 1971. Contends that Inge has delighted more audiences than Edward Albee and Tennessee Williams have.
Gassner, John. *Theatre at the Crossroads.* New York: Holt, Rinehart & Winston, 1960. Calls *Dark* "a group play . . . excellently orchestrated," but considers *Sheba* Inge's strongest play.

Gould, Jean. *Modern American Playwrights.* New York: Dodd, Mead, 1966, 264–72. A good overview of Inge's career through *Where's Daddy?*.

Kerr, Walter. *The Theatre in Spite of Itself.* New York: Simon & Schuster, 1963. Chiefly concerned with *Dark* and *Loss.*

Lewis, Allan. *American Plays and Playwrights of the Contemporary Theatre.* New York: Crown Publishers, 1965. Analyzes the reasons for Inge's decline after *Dark.* Compares *Bus Stop* to Gorki's *The Lower Depths.*

Newquist, Roy. *Counterpoint.* New York: Rand McNally, 1964. Contains biographical information about Inge.

Sievers, W. David. *Freud on Broadway.* New York: Hermitage House, 1955. Classifies *Sheba* and *Picnic* as naturalistic dramas.

Spoto, Donald. *The Kindness of Strangers: The Life of Tennessee Williams.* Boston: Little, Brown & Co., 1985. The best consideration of the Williams–Inge personal and artistic relationship.

Weales, Gerald. *American Drama Since World War II.* New York: Harcourt, Brace & World, 1962. One of the most valuable and perceptive early considerations of Inge's plays from *Sheba* to *Loss.*

———. *The Jumping-off Place: American Drama in the 1960's.* New York: Macmillan, 1969. Contrasts Inge to Edward Albee.

Williams, Tennessee. *Memoirs.* Garden City, N.Y.: Doubleday & Co., 1975. Frequent references to Inge and to his development as a playwright.

———. *Tennessee Williams's Letters to Donald Windham, 1940–1965.* New York: Holt, Rinehart & Winston, 1977. Shows Williams's shifting feelings about Inge over two and half decades.

Wood, Audrey, with Max Wilk. *Represented by Audrey Wood.* Garden City, N.Y.: Doubleday & Co., 1981. Sound insights into Inge's artistic life during the years that Wood was his agent.

Special Issue of Periodical *Kansas Quarterly* 18:4 (1986). Articles included in this issue devoted to Inge are annotated below.

Articles

Adler, Thomas K. "The School of Bill: An Inquiry into Literary Kinship (William Inge, Robert Anderson, and Arthur Laurents)." *Kansas Quarterly* 18, no. 4 (1986):113–20. A comparative view of Inge that seeks to demonstrate the uses of source material.

Anderson, Phyllis. "Diary of a Production." *Theatre Arts* 44 (November 1959):58–59. Surveys the course of *Sheba's* production.

Armato, Philip M. "The Bum as Scapegoat in William Inge's *Picnic*." *Western American Literature* 10 (Winter 1976):273–82. Analyzes the small-town syndrome by focusing on the way Hal is treated.

Bailey, Jeffrey. "William Inge: An Appreciation in Retrospect." *Kansas Quarterly* 18:4 (1986):139–47. Analyzes what happened to account for Inge's fall from popular acceptance.

Balch, Jack. "Anatomy of a Failure." *Theatre Arts* 44 (February 1960):10–13. Relates Inge biographically to the failure of *Loss*.

Brustein, Robert. "The Men-Taming Women of William Inge: *The Dark at the Top of the Stairs*." *Harper's,* November 1958, 52–57. A shattering commentary and vicious, not always accurate, attack on Inge's first four plays and on Inge as playwright.

Burgess, Charles E. "An American Experience: William Inge in St. Louis, 1943–1949." *Papers on Language and Literature* 12 (1976):438–68. A well-documented, carefully presented consideration of Inge's years in St. Louis, of his newspaper work, of his teaching at Washington University, and of his early relationship with Tennessee Williams.

Centola, Steven R. "Compromise as Bad Faith: Arthur Miller's *A View from the Bridge* and William Inge's *Come Back, Little Sheba*." *Midwest Quarterly* 28, no. 1 (Autumn 1986):100–113. A shrewd and valuable comparative study of two protagonists, Miller's Eddie Carbone and Inge's Doc Delaney.

Chandler, Laura. "Independence Honors Inge: The William Inge Festival." *Kansas Quarterly* 18, no. 4 (1986):149–53. Tells of the establishment of the Inge Collection at Independence Community College in Kansas.

Clurman, Harold. "A Good Play." *New Republic,* 13 March 1950, 22–23. Presents the criteria for a good play and fits Inge's *Sheba* to these criteria.

Driver, Tom F. "Hearts and Heads." *Christian Century,* 1 January 1958, 17–18. Defends *Dark* as Inge's best play since *Sheba*.

Gale, Steven H. "Small Town Images in Four Plays by William Inge." *Kansas Quarterly* 18, no. 4 (1986):89–102. Demonstrates the authenticity of Inge's observations of small-town life in the Midwest.

Gibbs, Wolcott. "The Crowded Stairway." *New Yorker,* 14 December 1957, 83–85. Focuses on *Dark* and commends Inge for his infallible ear and controlled style.

Hamblet, Edwin. "The North American Outlook of Marcel Dube and William Inge." *Queen's Quarterly* 77, no. 3 (Autumn 1970):374–87. Likens Dube to Arthur Miller, Tennessee Williams, and William Inge, but thinks the greatest similarity is to Inge.

Hayes, Richard. "A Question of Reality." *Commonweal,* 14 March 1958, 615–16. Notes the pleasure of recognition *Dark* imparts.

Herron, Ira Honaker. "Our Vanishing Towns: Modern Broadway Versions." *Southwest Review* 51, no. 3 (Summer 1966):209–20. Considers Inge's depiction of midwestern towns from *Sheba* to *Loss*.

Juhnke, Janet. "Inge's Women: Robert Brustein and the Feminine Mystique." *Kansas Quarterly* 18, no. 4 (1986):103–12. Analyzes Inge's attitudes toward women from a feminist point of view and contests Brustein's contentions.

Knudsen, James. "Last Words: The Novels of William Inge." *Kansas Quarterly* 18, no. 4 (1986):121–28. Finds strong dramatic elements in Inge's two novels.

Lange, Jane W. " 'Forces Get Loose': Social Prophecy in William Inge's *Picnic*." *Kansas Quarterly* 18, no. 4 (1986):57–70. Shows Inge against the popular social context of the 1950s.

Lewis, Theophilus. "Theatre." *America*, 2 May 1953, 147. Is dismayed at Inge's receiving the New York Drama Critics' Award for *Picnic*.

McIlrath, Patricia. "William Inge, Great Voice of the Heart of America." *Kansas Quarterly* 18, no. 4 (1986):45–53. Writes of Inge's truth and honesty in presenting middle America.

Miller, Jordan Y. "William Inge: Last of the Realists?" *Kansas Quarterly* 2, no. 2 (Spring 1970):17–26. Points out that Inge works better with people than with themes, causes, or regional color.

Mitchell, Marilyn. "The Teacher as Outsider in the Works of William Inge." *Midwest Quarterly* 17 (1976):385–93. Considers Inge's view of the teaching profession.

————. "William Inge." *American Imago* 35 (1978):297–310. A psychological consideration of Inge and his work.

Scheick, William J. "Self and the Art of Memory in Inge's *My Son Is a Splendid Driver*." *Kansas Quarterly* 18, no. 4 (1986):131–37. Sees Inge's final novel in its autobiographical perspective.

Steele, Lloyd. "William Inge: The Last Interview." *Los Angeles Free Press*, 22 June 1973, 18–22. Steele's interview with Inge two weeks before his death shows Inge's depression at his perception that he could no longer write.

Voss, Ralph F. "William Inge and the Savior/Specter of Celebrity." *Kansas Quarterly* 18, no. 4 (1986):25–40. Contains interesting comments from people who knew Inge in various contexts during his lifetime.

Wentworth, Michael. "The Convergence of Fairy Tale and Myth in William Inge's *Picnic*." *Kansas Quarterly* 18, no. 4 (1986):75–85. Elaborates on the personal fantasies of Inge's characters and relates them to a broader context.

Wood, Michael. "An Interview with Daniel Mann (The Director of Inge's First Success and His First Failure)." *Kansas Quarterly* 18, no. 4 (1986):7–22. Mann comments on Inge's career and on the success of *Sheba* and failure of *Loss*.

Index